# THE VERY BEST
# SALMON
## COOKBOOK

JOHN NICOLAS

BRISTOL PUBLISHING ENTERPRISES
Hayward, California

# A nitty gritty® cookbook

Printed in the United States of America.

ISBN 1-55867-321-0

Cover design: Frank J. Paredes
Cover photography: John Benson
Food stylist: Randy Mon
Illustrations: Nora Wylde

# CONTENTS

*1*    A Brief Course in Salmon Types
*3*    Buying, Handling and Storing Salmon
*6*    Smoked and Cured Salmon
*10*    Hot-Smoking Salmon at Home
*13*    Appetizers and Hors d'Oeuvres
*35*    Salads and Pasta
*47*    Entrées
*122*    Marinades and Sauces
*152*    Index

# ACKNOWLEDGMENTS

Special thanks go to my wife, Barbara, for her love and support. Thanks to her dedication to excellence, she helped me develop some of the new dishes that appear here and made a crucial editorial pass over most of the written recipes in first-draft form.

My deep appreciation to a wonderful Canadian team: Susan Hayes, Jill Geraghty and Alice Montgomery. Their culinary skills and concrete support were invaluable. They helped me to innovate and develop my personal style. I also acknowledge the collaboration of Barbara, Diane, Elaine, Gladys, Linda, Patsy and Teresa.

As a salmon fisherman, with over thirty most enjoyable summers teasing wild salmon on the magnificent Cascapedia River in Québec, Canada, I was fortunate to be surrounded by the finest managing and guiding team, making every season a rewarding one in which to tackle the King of Fish. My thanks go to Conrad, Ricky, Jerry, Ronny, and Jeffrey Legouffe, Terry Barter, Danny Sexton, Yves Bujold, Real Bujold, Dana Willett, Vern Lebrecque, Jeremiah Sexton and Mark Stone, Hammond Mc Cormack and Ralph Willett.

I also thank Bob Bujold and Harry Best for their great managerial support.

# A BRIEF COURSE IN SALMON TYPES

I would like to share with you my enormous pleasure in discovering the unique fish that is salmon. This book covers buying, handling, storing, preparation and cooking techniques for salmon. A thorough analysis guides the reader through the best means of buying and smoking salmon. Most of the book consists of salmon recipes. Many of the dishes can be prepared in a short time, or hours in advance.

## THE SPECIES OF SALMON

There are two main varieties of salmon species: **Atlantic** and **Pacific**. Although they are genetically almost identical, historically they do not interbreed.

**Atlantic** salmon is native to the northern Atlantic Ocean and rivers that flow into the Atlantic. It differs from Pacific salmon only in that it can spawn more than once. Atlantic salmon, among all species of salmon, is the most suitable for smoking .

There are five main species of **Pacific** salmon: Chinook, or King; Coho, or Silver; Sockeye; Chum; and Pink.

**Chinook,** or **King** salmon, accounts for about 20 percent of the total salmon fished in the Pacific and is one of the most commercially valuable fish in the world. Suitable for most recipes, Chinook salmon is often used for smoking.

**Coho,** or **Silver** salmon, run 12–18 lbs. and is considered by many to be the best salmon for barbecues. They have a firm bright red flesh, with a mild flavor.

**Sockeye** salmon, with its deep red flesh, is the smallest of the Pacific salmon, and for its rich flavor, the most sought-after variety.

**Chum** salmon is similar to Sockeye, with a milder and more delicate flavor.

**Pink** salmon are the most plentiful of all Pacific salmon species, with a mild flavor and light flesh color.

**Steelhead** salmon are genetically almost identical to native American trout, also known as **Rainbow trout**. Steelhead grow much larger than Rainbow trout, however.

**Arctic Char, Brook** trout and **Lake** trout are all part of the salmon and trout family. The flesh of Arctic char can be anywhere from dark red to quite pale pink. Brook trout are very popular with anglers. The rarer Lake trout are the largest of all the trout species.

## SALMON AND HEALTH

Salmon is an excellent source of vitamin A, vitamin D, niacin, riboflavin and other B group vitamins. It also has a high content of the water-soluble vitamins $B_{12}$ and pyridoxine.

While fish-oil supplements get the press, the health benefits of the original source of the oil should not be overlooked. Fish is a very lean alternative to red meat: 3 ounces of cooked Atlantic salmon has less than one-third the total fat of 3 ounces of broiled rib-eye steak.

Not only is fish low in fat, but it has become common knowledge that the kind of fat it contains—omega-3 fatty acids, the working components of fish oil—is good for your heart.

Researchers agree that omega-3s lower the liver's production of triglycerides, a particularly bad type of blood fat. Also, omega-3s seem to reduce the tendency of blood to form clots. In general, eating fish 2 to 3 times a week is a heart-smart choice.

CONCERNS OF CONTAMINANTS IN SALMON

Although current evidence suggests that contaminants in salmon do not pose a threat to human health, over the past years reports of PCBs in farmed and wild salmon have raised concerns about the health benefits of the species. PCBs are ubiquitous in the environment, and occur in many foods, including beef, milk and chicken. The PCB intake in the diet of the average American comes mainly from other foods, not salmon—farmed or wild.

Food producers are addressing this issue, and now consumers can buy organically farmed salmon raised on food without PCBs.

The data show quite convincingly that regardless of whether the salmon are farm bred or caught wild, the amounts of these chemicals are small indeed, about 100 times lower than the safe amounts recommended by the US FDA's health-based risk assessments.

# BUYING, HANDLING AND STORING SALMON

**Drawn** salmon are whole, cleaned salmon. They need to be scaled and washed before cooking. **Dressed** and **pan-dressed** salmon are both scaled and eviscerated. Usually, head, tail, and fins are removed. **Steaks** are cross-section slices of larger dressed salmon. They are ready to cook as purchased. Look for center cuts, as steaks from the tail end are small and not appealing. **Fillets** are the sides of dressed salmon, cut lengthwise away from the backbones. Fillets may be skinned, and require no preparation before cooking. **Butterfly fillets** are the sides of the salmon held together by the uncut belly skin or by the back. **Salmon roast** is the center cut of dressed salmon. Choose salmon roasts in sizes to meet your specific needs.

## BUYING FRESH SALMON

To ensure you're buying the freshest fish, look for these details:

- The odor is sea-fresh and mild. (Fresh salmon, whether wild or farmed, has practically no "fishy" smell.)
- The flesh is firm and elastic when subjected to finger pressure. (Farmed salmon has a less resilient texture than the wild species.)
- In buying fillets and steaks, look for a fresh-cut appearance, and color ranging from pink to red. In a whole fish, the eyes are bright, clean, transparent and full. The skin is shiny and bright in color. Wrinkles should not remain when fish is bent slightly. The scales are shiny and adhere tightly to the skin.
- Salmon cut into fillets or steaks should be displayed on ice. Fresh salmon steaks and fillets should be firm, moist and rosy in color.

Refrigerate fresh salmon just after purchase and cook it within the day. Before cooking, check for pin bones by rubbing your finger over salmon; pull them out with clean tweezers, rinse salmon under cold water, and dry with paper towels.

## HANDLING AND STORING SALMON

Fresh whole salmon should be refrigerated on ice as soon as it is received. It should not be exposed to air unnecessarily as oxidation may alter the flavor. Fillets or steaks lose their flavor more rapidly than whole fish and should be processed without delay.

Smoked salmon should not be placed in contact with ice, and should be double-wrapped and stored in an airtight container to control its penetrating odors.

Salmon to be frozen should be wrapped and sealed in moisture- and vapor-proof material. Do not freeze salmon that is wrapped only in waxed paper or plastic wrap.

## HOW TO FREEZE OR GLAZE SALMON

Fresh salmon may be frozen in a block of ice or by glazing, both of which prevent moisture loss. To freeze salmon in a block of ice, place the fish in a container large enough to hold the fish and cover with water, then freeze until solid.

Glazing is as effective as block freezing and takes less freezer space. To glaze salmon, place in a single layer on a tray, wrap and freeze. As soon as the fish is completely frozen, remove from the freezer, unwrap, and dip quickly in ice-cold water. A glaze will form immediately. Repeat the dipping process 3 or 4 times. A thick coating of ice will result from each dipping. If necessary, return the fish to the freezer between dips if the glaze does not build up after 2 or 3 dips. Handle the salmon carefully to avoid breaking the glaze. When glazed, wrap the salmon tightly in freezer wrap or aluminum foil and return to the freezer. Glazing may need to be repeated if the fish is not used within 1 or 2 months.

Good quality salmon will keep about 3 months if handled correctly from catch to freezer. Commercially packaged frozen salmon should be placed in a freezer in its original wrapper immediately after purchase to maintain quality. Store at 0° or lower. It is a good practice to date packages for easy rotation.

## SMOKED AND CURED SALMON

Before the arrival of cold storage and refrigeration, salmon was preserved by smoking and curing in brine. Salmon smoking relies on the basic processes of curing and drying. Both inhibit spoilage and growth of bacteria by reducing the moisture in the fish. Today, the choices in smoked and cured salmons are endless.

One general rule to remember: Hot-smoked salmon is cooked during the smoking process, while cold-smoked salmon is preserved in its raw state. Here are some guidelines to sorting out the many varieties of smoked salmon:

**KIPPERED OR HOT-SMOKED:** The salmon is cured in a brine solution and smoked at high temperatures. It is moist, tender and flaky, with a strong smoked flavor. The Pacific King salmon species are often used. A coating of cracked black peppercorns transforms kippered salmon into "pastrami salmon." Packaged in whole sides or chunks, the refrigeration shelf life of kippered or hot-smoked salmon will vary according to the concentration of salt and the use of preservatives. Refrigerate kippered salmon for a week to 10 days, or freeze for an extended storage period. The special slow hot-smoking process renders the salmon amazingly tender and moist.

**LOX OR NOVA LOX:** Lox, also known as Nova lox or belly lox, is a popular processing method generally prepared from Pacific species. The fish is cured in brine, and soaked to remove salt. It may be lightly smoked at very low temperatures. Sometimes, it may contain food coloring. Lox is inexpensive and often salty. When "lox style" is used to describe smoked salmon today, it is likely to refer to a salty fish.

**NOVA OR NOVA SCOTIA:** Nova or Nova Scotia smoked salmon refers to a method of mild curing and cold smoking; the term Nova or Novi is also used to refer to any smoked salmon regardless the source. The quality varies according to the salmon and the smoking process. Frequently vacuum-packed, this variety can be found thinly sliced or as whole smoked sides.

**WILD WESTERN NOVA:** This is a wild king salmon from the Pacific. Its lean body has very little fat and captures the light wood smoke wonderfully. The wild fish, belly-cut, is usually wet cured, and is leaner and firmer than farmed fish.

**WILD BALTIC:** Caught seasonally between Denmark and Sweden; smoked in Denmark. It is pale and earthy, with a peat-like flavor. It varies in taste, texture, smokiness and saltiness.

**SCANDINAVIAN GRAVLAX WITH DILL:** Gravlaks or gravlax is not smoked, but cured and coated in a delicate brine of salt, sugar and dill. Goes best with a touch of mustard sauce.

**SCOTTISH, IRISH, NORWEGIAN AND ICELANDIC:** The finest wild Atlantic salmon from these regions have been fished for many years. The sides of wild or farmed Atlantic salmon from those countries are cured and cold-smoked, using nothing but natural ingredients. It is the smoking that gives the salmon the distinctive, soft aroma of wood smoke and its unique silky texture and flavor: lean, firm, a little salty.

**DRIED SALMON OR SALMON JERKY:** The combination of both the lox and kippered salmon processing methods is used to make dried salmon or salmon jerky. Pacific salmon is cut into strips, soaked in a brine and slow-smoked for an extended period. One style is very smoky and moist. Another, sometimes called squaw candy, is cut into strips, smoked and dried until rubbery, with a firm and chewy texture, like beef jerky.

**RETORT POUCH OR CANNED SMOKED SALMON:** is a brined, lightly smoked salmon which is packed in either a foil laminated vacuum pouch or can. The pouch or can is then vacuum sealed and sterilized (retorted) through pressure cooking to ensure a stable shelf life without refrigeration.

## THE ART OF BUYING SMOKED SALMON

Judging smoked salmon and analyzing its quality are not easy matters. Today, the salmon which sets the standard by which all smoked salmon is judged comes from Scotland. At its best, smoked salmon is rosy-pink, silky, tender, mild, and appetizing, with a subtle smoke flavor. A moderate amount of salt enhances but does not block its refined quality. The Scottish smoked salmon producers are among the best in the world, and are proud and very protective of their industry. Genuine smoked Scottish salmon is a salmon caught or farmed in Scotland that has also been smoked in Scotland. Some other producers identify their product as "Scottish smoked salmon," meaning that their salmon is smoked (regardless of source) in the "Scottish style." Look for the "Scottish Salmon — Smoked in Scotland" Quality Mark, to identify genuine smoked Scottish salmon if you want to try the real thing.

Norwegians also produce consistently good quality smoked salmon. Norwegian smoked salmon are fattier than Scottish salmon. The flesh is rich, and often tender and soft, like the Nova or Nova Scotia.

Irish smoked salmon has a more intense smoke flavor than the Scottish and Norwegian smoked salmon. It is "hard cured," which means that the salmon has a drier texture. It is meatier and less fatty.

Although Switzerland does not produce any salmon, Atlantic salmon from Norwegian and Russian origins are smoked in this country. Salmon is cured and exposed to mild hardwood smoke. In addition, herbs are often burned to produce a smoked salmon of exceptional high standard.

The Pacific Northwest of the United States and British Columbia produce hot -smoked and kippered Chinook and Coho salmon. The bright orange Copper River king salmon from Alaska is often cold-smoked, producing a good quality product.

There is a wide range of color variations in fine quality smoked salmon. Scottish, Norwegian, Icelandic and Canadian smoked salmon have a medium-pale orange color; avoid intense pinks and reds. Smoked salmon experts always look for a creamy-silky texture with a satisfying amount of fish oil. You should avoid smoked salmon that is too fatty or oily, too soft and mushy, too hard or dry, or bruised and discolored.

In an ideal world, it's best to purchase fish within 24 hours after it has been smoked. However, refrigerated, smoked salmon will be fine for a week. If you're in doubt, ask when it was smoked.

## HOT-SMOKING SALMON AT HOME

Hot-smoking salmon at home can be a rewarding experience. Unlike the time-consuming cold smoking process, hot-smoking gives rapid results. The art of hot-smoking lies in controlling the heat and the curing process. Hot-smoked salmon is fully cooked and should be consumed within a few days, or frozen.

First cure the salmon: simply sprinkle salt directly on the salmon. Allow about 1 tablespoon salt per pound of boneless salmon. A mixture of salt and sugar in a proportion of 5 to 1 will give a mellower taste. Apply a heavier layer of the salt or salt-sugar cure on the thickest part of the fillet and a little less on the thinner tail and belly, so that the cure will be more evenly distributed. Cover and refrigerate for 8 hours or overnight.

Before smoking, drain liquid that has collected around fish. Cover salmon with cold water. Let stand for 15 minutes, drain and repeat. Pat dry. Lay fillet on a rack and dry for up to 2 hours in a breezy place.

Brining is another easy way to cure salmon for hot-smoking. Use about 2 tbs. total salt and sugar per cup of cold water. Measure enough cold water to cover salmon. Depending on the size, allow fish to steep in brine for 2 to 4 hours under refrigeration. Thinner fillets require less time in the brine than large thick fillets. Rinse salmon in fresh cold water and hang or lay on a rack in a cool breezy place to dry for 2 to 3 hours. The outer surface of fish will dry into a thin pellicle, which gives a good appearance to the finished fish and helps slow the loss of moisture as it smokes.

### HOT-SMOKING WITH A GRILL

Start a charcoal fire in a covered grill, and let it cook down until the coals are not fiery hot. Add moistened hardwood chips or fruitwood cuttings for smoke. The key is to control the temperature of the covered grill to around 180° to 200° during smoking of the salmon. To check temperature, insert an instant-reading thermometer through the vent hole of the kettle.

Lay salmon skin side down on a rack that will fit in the grill. Place in the center of the grill. Cover and close bottom and top vents about 90 percent. Smoke fish for 30 to 40 minutes or until flesh goes from translucent to opaque. Test the center with a skewer. Cool smoked salmon, then wrap and refrigerate before serving.

## SMOKING IN A WOK

Stovetop smoking in a wok can be very rewarding. (The use of a cast-iron skillet is also possible; see *Pan-Smoked Salmon,* page 55).

Marinate pieces of boneless fresh salmon in soy sauce and ginger for up to 1 hour. Other exotic spices can be added to flavor the fish. The smoke source is a mixture of equal parts raw rice, brown sugar and black tea leaves. Wood chips or sawdust are also good alternatives for wok smoking.

For best results, use a wok 14 inches in diameter or larger with a tight-fitting lid, and a rack that will fit inside. Line the inside of the wok with a sheet of heavy-duty foil, letting the excess drape over the pan. Combine rice, sugar and tea and spread on the foil in the bottom of the wok. Put the wire rack in place and turn the heat to high. Meanwhile, drain and dry salmon pieces.

When sugar begins to burn, place fish on the rack. Cover the wok, folding the foil over the lid. Reduce heat to medium and cook fish for 10 to 15 minutes. Use an exhaust fan if possible as some smoke will leak from the wok. Remove the lid and test the fish for doneness by checking the thickest part with a skewer. The center should be opaque. Take the wok outdoors if possible, so that the smoke will not set off any indoor alarm.

Serve salmon hot or cold. If smoking with a wok becomes a habit, it may be a good idea to dedicate one wok for smoking.

# APPETIZERS AND HORS D'OEUVRES

14 Gravlax
15 Smoked Salmon Bagelettes
16 Smoked Salmon Quesadillas
17 Smoked Salmon Bruschetta on Rye
18 Smoked Salmon Tartare
19 Smoked Salmon with Cucumber
     Salad
20 Stuffed Cucumbers
21 Blinis
22 Potato Galettes with Smoked Salmon
     and Dill Crème Fraîche

24 Smoked Salmon Corncakes
25 Smoked Salmon Spirals
26 Grilled Salmon Skewers
27 Smoked Salmon Spread with Capers
28 Cold Salmon Mousse
29 Rillettes of Salmon
30 Smoked Salmon Terrine
31 Salmon Shrimp Terrine
32 Terrine of Salmon
34 Salmon-Stuffed Eggs

# GRAVLAX

*Dill Mustard Sauce, page 138, is a classic accompaniment, as are rye bread and cucumber slices.*

1 salmon fillet (2½ lb.)
¼ cup salt
¼ cup sugar
10 fresh dill sprigs, divided

1 medium onion, thinly sliced
1 tbs. cracked peppercorns
¼ cup cognac, optional
capers, for garnish

Extract all bones from the fillet. Mix salt and sugar in a small bowl. Rub salt mixture into the fleshy side of salmon. Spread half of the dill in a glass or ceramic dish. Place salmon skin side down on top of the dill in the dish. Sprinkle onion and peppercorns over salmon. Pour cognac, if using, over salmon. Sprinkle remaining dill over fish. Cover dish with plastic wrap. Place a board on top of dish so that it presses on the wrapped fish. Put about a 5-pound weight on top of board (cans of food will work well). Refrigerate fish for 2 to 3 days, basting salmon with the marinade once or twice a day.

Before serving, remove dill and onion from the top of the salmon and discard. Place fillet skin side down on a cutting board. Slice the fillet on the diagonal into thin strips, freeing them from the skin. Roll the thin slices. Garnish with capers.

# SMOKED SALMON BAGELETTES

*An elegant version of bagels with cream cheese and lox, these bagelettes are perfect for brunch or as an hors d'oeuvre.*

10 miniature bagels, split
8 oz. cream cheese, softened
4 oz. smoked salmon (hot- or cold-smoked)

1 tbs. chopped fresh chives
1 tbs. chopped fresh dill, for garnish

Toast bagel halves; set aside. In a food processor workbowl, blend cream cheese, smoked salmon and chives into a creamy consistency. Spoon into a pastry bag fitted with a star tip and pipe salmon mixture on bagels, or mound salmon mixture on bagels with a spoon. Garnish with dill.

King Salmon

# SMOKED SALMON QUESADILLAS

*To make these low-fat, warm the tortillas in the oven or on a grill instead of frying them.*

4 oz. soft fresh goat cheese
2 tbs. grated horseradish, well drained
2 tbs. sour cream
3 tbs. chopped fresh dill, divided
salt and pepper to taste

5 tbs. olive oil
6 flour tortillas (7-inch)
12 thin slices cold-smoked salmon (about 8 oz.)
1 tbs. fresh lemon juice

Blend goat cheese, horseradish, sour cream and 1 tbs. of the dill in a small bowl. Season cheese mixture with salt and pepper. Set aside.

In a small skillet, heat oil over medium-high heat for 1 minute. Fry tortillas, 1 at a time, turning once, for 2 minutes, or until lightly browned. Drain on paper towels.

Spread 1 rounded tbs. cheese mixture over each tortilla. Top with smoked salmon and sprinkle with a pinch of the remaining dill. Cut quesadillas into quarters and drizzle with lemon juice. Serve immediately.

# SMOKED SALMON BRUSCHETTA ON RYE

*Rye or pumpernickel bread goes well with smoked salmon. This is a refreshing combination prepared with ease.*

3 thick slices rye bread
1 clove garlic, halved
4 oz. cold-smoked salmon, coarsely
    chopped
2 tbs. finely chopped red onion
1 tbs. chopped fresh dill

2 plum tomatoes, chopped
1 tbs. lemon juice
1 tbs. olive oil
salt and pepper to taste
sour cream and chopped fresh chives, for
    garnish

Lightly toast bread on both sides. Rub cut garlic over 1 side of each toast slice; set aside.

In a small bowl, combine salmon, onion, dill, tomatoes, lemon juice and olive oil. Season with salt and pepper if necessary. Spread mixture on garlic side of bread. Cut into bite-sized pieces. Garnish each with a dollop of sour cream and a sprinkle of chives.

# SMOKED SALMON TARTARE

*This simple recipe is suitable as hors d'oeuvres on toasts or Blinis, page 21, or as a first course, and can be prepared several hours ahead and kept in the refrigerator.*

$\frac{1}{2}$ lb. cold-smoked salmon
1 tbs. extra-virgin olive oil
1 tbs. small capers
3 tbs. minced fresh chives, divided
1 tbs. thinly sliced fresh basil, divided
pepper to taste
4 lime wedges, for garnish

Slice salmon and dice into about $\frac{1}{4}$-inch pieces. Mix with olive oil and capers in a small bowl. Add $\frac{1}{2}$ the chives and $\frac{1}{2}$ the basil. Season with pepper.

AS A FIRST COURSE: Divide salmon tartare evenly among 4 salad plates. Sprinkle remaining chives and basil on top. Season with more pepper to taste and garnish with lime wedges.

AS HORS D'OEUVRES: Mound a tsp. of the salmon tartare on small toast rounds or crackers. Sprinkle with remaining chives and basil. Season with more pepper. Serve cold.

# SMOKED SALMON WITH CUCUMBER SALAD

*The cool, creamy cucumber salad makes a sharp contrast to the rich smoked salmon.*

1 large seedless cucumber, peeled
salt
1/2 cup plain yogurt
1/2 cup sour cream
1 bunch fresh dill, finely chopped
2 tbs. chopped fresh mint, or 1 tsp. dried

1 tsp. minced garlic
juice of 1/2 lemon
pepper to taste
3 pita breads, toasted
18 slices (about 8 oz.) cold-smoked salmon

Halve cucumber lengthwise, remove seeds and shred cucumber, using a food processor fitted with a shredding disk or on the large holes of a box grater. Place cucumber in a sieve, sprinkle generously with salt and place over a bowl. Set aside for at least 30 minutes.

Rinse cucumber well under cold water and wrap in a clean towel. Wring out moisture. Place cucumber in a bowl. Add yogurt, sour cream, dill, mint, garlic, lemon juice and pepper and mix well. Cover and refrigerate for at least 15 minutes but no longer than 2 hours.

Cut pita breads into 6 wedges each. Drape 1 slice of salmon onto each piece of bread, and spoon cucumber salad on top.

# STUFFED CUCUMBERS

*Serve these pretty salmon/cucumber slices on rounds of buttered pumpernickel bread.*

2 medium seedless cucumbers
8 oz. smoked salmon (hot- or cold-smoked)
4 oz. cream cheese, softened
$1/2$ cup (1 stick) butter, softened
1 tbs. Dijon mustard
1 tbs. lemon juice

Cut cucumbers lengthwise in half. Scoop out seeds and discard. Set cucumber halves aside.

Combine smoked salmon with cream cheese, butter, mustard and lemon juice in a food processor workbowl and process into a paste. Fill cavities of cucumber halves with salmon mixture. Place halves together to resemble a whole cucumber. Wrap and refrigerate for 1 hour.

Slice stuffed cucumbers into $1/2$-inch rounds. Serve cold.

# BLINIS

*Blinis are small, light pancakes that can be prepared days ahead and frozen. They are served as appetizers or hors d'oeuvres and topped with smoked salmon,* Rillettes of Salmon, page 29, *or a simple combination of sour cream and salmon caviar.*

1½ cups milk, divided
1½ tsp. active dry yeast
1 cup all-purpose flour
1 cup buckwheat flour
3 egg yolks

1 tsp. salt
3 egg whites
½ tsp. cream of tartar
vegetable oil, for cooking

Heat 1 cup of the milk in microwave until it is warm. Dissolve yeast in warm milk. Place flours in a large bowl and make a well in the center. Add the milk-yeast mixture, egg yolks and salt. Mix well. Cover bowl and leave to rise at room temperature until doubled in volume, about 1 hour. Stir in remaining ½ cup milk. Beat egg whites with cream of tartar in a medium bowl until stiff. Fold into batter.

Heat a large nonstick skillet over medium heat. Brush pan with oil. Pour about 1 tbs. batter into pan for each blini and cook until golden, 2 to 3 minutes on each side. Transfer to a tray. Cover with foil. Repeat with remaining batter. Serve blinis hot or at room temperature.

# POTATO GALETTES WITH SMOKED SALMON AND DILL CRÈME FRAÎCHE

*Individual potato pancakes called galettes are topped with a sour cream mixture and smoked salmon. The potato galettes can be browned 2 hours in advance, then baked in the oven 10 minutes before serving.*

¼ cup crème fraîche or sour cream
3 tbs. minced shallots or onions
2 tbs. minced fresh dill, or 2 tsp. dried
1½ tbs. lemon juice, divided
salt and pepper to taste

2 large Idaho potatoes
¼ cup (½ stick) butter, melted
4 oz. cold-smoked salmon, thinly sliced
3 tbs. salmon caviar, optional, for garnish
1 tbs. minced fresh chives, for garnish

Arctic Char

Heat oven to 400°. Mix crème fraîche, shallots, dill and 1 tbs. of the lemon juice in a bowl. Season with salt and pepper. Cover and refrigerate until ready to use. (Mixture can be prepared a day ahead. Keep refrigerated.)

Peel and finely grate potatoes. Rinse potatoes under cold water and drain well. Toss potatoes with 2 tbs. of the butter in a bowl. Season with salt and pepper.

Heat a large cast iron skillet over high heat. Add remaining 2 tbs. butter. Spoon ½ cupfuls of grated potatoes in skillet to make 4 round galettes. Press and flatten potatoes into pancakes. Cook 2 minutes. Reduce heat to medium-high and cook until bottom is golden, about 4 minutes.

Flip galettes and cook until second sides are golden, about 4 minutes. Transfer pan to oven; cook until galettes are crisp, about 10 minutes.

Spread galettes with crème fraîche. Top with salmon. Drizzle with lemon juice and season with pepper. Garnish with caviar, if using, and chives.

# SMOKED SALMON CORNCAKES

*The spicy smoked salmon corncakes are cooked in a skillet, and served as a brunch entrée or appetizers with sour cream, chopped red onion and lemon slices.*

3/4 cup yellow cornmeal
6 tbs. flour
1/2 tsp. baking soda
1/2 tsp. salt
2 eggs
3/4 cup buttermilk
6 tbs. cream cheese, softened

1 cup fresh corn or frozen corn, thawed
6 tbs. finely chopped fresh chives
1 tsp. finely chopped jalapeño pepper
1 cup finely chopped smoked salmon (hot- or cold-smoked)
1/4 cup vegetable oil

In a medium bowl, combine cornmeal, flour, baking soda and salt. In a large bowl, whisk together eggs, buttermilk and cream cheese. Chop half of the corn coarsely and stir into buttermilk mixture with remaining corn, chives, jalapeño pepper, salmon and cornmeal mixture until just combined.

In a large nonstick skillet heat oil over medium heat. Drop batter by 1/4-cupfuls into skillet. Spread batter slightly to form 3- to 4-inch cakes and cook for 2 to 3 minutes on each side, or until golden brown. Serve warm.

# SMOKED SALMON SPIRALS

*These beautiful pink and white spirals can also be served with toast rounds or crackers.*

8 oz. cold-smoked salmon, thinly sliced
8 oz. cream cheese, softened
1 tbs. chopped fresh dill, or 1 tsp. dried
1 tbs. tiny capers, drained
1 seedless cucumber, sliced ¼-inch thick

Arrange smoked salmon slices, overlapping slightly, on a sheet of plastic wrap in a 12 by 8-inch rectangle.

Mix cream cheese with dill in a small bowl; spread over smoked salmon. Sprinkle capers over cream cheese mixture. Roll up smoked salmon jelly roll-style to form a cylinder. Enclose in plastic wrap. Refrigerate for several hours, until the cylinder is firm.

Thinly slice the smoked salmon roll, and arrange on cucumber slices.

# GRILLED SALMON SKEWERS

*These skewers are quick and delicious appetizers, or serve three or four skewers per guest as an entrée, with rice and stir-fried vegetables.*

1/4 cup soy sauce
1/4 cup honey
1 tbs. rice vinegar
1 tsp. minced fresh ginger
1 clove garlic, minced
1 pinch pepper
1 lb. salmon fillet, boned and skinned
1 lemon, cut in 12 wedges, optional

In a bowl, whisk together soy sauce, honey, vinegar, ginger, garlic and pepper; set aside. Slice salmon lengthwise into 12 long strips. Thread each strip onto a wooden skewer. Place in a shallow dish. Pour soy sauce mixture over skewers, turning to coat well. Marinate at room temperature for 30 minutes. Prepare a medium-hot grill.

Thread 1 lemon wedge, if using, onto end of each skewer. Grill skewers on an oiled grill rack, brushing often with marinade, for 4 minutes on 1 side; turn and grill for 3 to 4 minutes, or until fish flakes easily.

# SMOKED SALMON SPREAD WITH CAPERS

*This fast and elegant appetizer can be made several hours ahead. Serve with crackers or slices of French bread.*

1 cup chopped smoked salmon (hot- or cold-smoked)
6 oz. cream cheese, softened
1 tsp. lemon juice
1 tbs. milk
1 tbs. capers, rinsed and drained
½ tsp. *Fish Seasoning*, page 43

Combine smoked salmon, cream cheese, lemon juice, milk, capers and *Fish Seasoning* in a food processor workbowl. Process until smooth. Transfer to a bowl. Cover with plastic wrap and refrigerate until ready to serve.

# COLD SALMON MOUSSE

*Serve this with toasts or crackers and garnish with lemon wedges. Salmon mousse can also be used as a filling for tomatoes, cucumbers, artichoke bottoms or mushroom caps.*

1 tbs. unflavored gelatin powder
1/2 cup cold water
1/2 cup mayonnaise
salt and pepper to taste
1 tsp. Worcestershire sauce
1/4 tsp. cayenne pepper

2 tsp. chopped fresh dill
1/4 tsp. paprika
1 tbs. lemon juice
2 cups cooked salmon, boned and skinned
1 cup heavy cream

In a small saucepan off heat, dissolve gelatin in water. Set aside for 5 minutes. Place saucepan over low heat. Heat, stirring, until gelatin is melted. Pour into a bowl and cool to room temperature. Whisk in mayonnaise, salt, pepper, Worcestershire, cayenne, dill, paprika and lemon juice. Refrigerate for 15 to 20 minutes until mixture begins to thicken lightly.

Blend salmon in a food processor workbowl until finely chopped. In a small bowl, whisk cream until soft peaks form. Fold salmon and cream into gelatin mixture. Transfer mousse to a large mold or individual molds and refrigerate for 3 to 4 hours to set.

Just before serving, dip mold in warm water for a few seconds. Invert on a platter.

# RILLETTES OF SALMON

*The combination of fresh and smoked salmon, well seasoned with a variety of condiments and herbs, bring a rich flavor to this hors d'oeuvre. Can be prepared a day in advance. Recipe can be doubled.*

8 oz. fresh cooked salmon
8 oz. cold-smoked salmon, finely diced
1 tsp. minced shallot or onion
1/2 cup (1 stick) butter, softened
1/4 cup chopped fresh parsley
1 tbs. lemon juice
1 tsp. Dijon mustard

1 tsp. capers
1 tsp. cognac
1 tsp. grated lemon zest
1/4 tsp. pepper
8 slices pumpernickel bread, or
4 dozen *Blinis*, page 21

Remove any skin or bones from fresh salmon. Put in a food processor workbowl and process to a smooth paste. Add smoked salmon, shallots, butter, parsley, lemon juice, mustard, capers, cognac, lemon zest and pepper. Pulse until smooth.

Spoon salmon mixture into a serving bowl. Refrigerate for 1 hour. Serve with thin slices of pumpernickel or *Blinis*.

# SMOKED SALMON TERRINE

*This dish may be prepared a day in advance. Serve the terrine with slices of French bread, or on a bed of dressed salad greens as a first course.*

1 lb. fresh spinach, stems removed
4 oz. cream cheese, softened
½ cup (1 stick) butter, softened
1 tbs. Worcestershire sauce

½ tsp. Tabasco Sauce
salt and pepper to taste
1 lb. cold-smoked salmon, thinly sliced

Cook spinach in salted boiling water for 3 to 4 minutes. Plunge spinach in ice water. Drain and squeeze dry. Combine spinach, cream cheese, butter, Worcestershire and Tabasco in a food processor workbowl. Process to a smooth paste. Season with salt and pepper.

Lightly butter the sides of a 1½-qt. terrine or large loaf pan. Line the mold with plastic wrap. Cover bottom and sides of terrine with 1 layer of smoked salmon. Spread a ½-inch layer of spinach mixture in the bottom of the terrine and smooth evenly. Arrange a layer of smoked salmon over spinach mixture. Continue to alternate layers of spinach and salmon, ending with salmon. Cover with plastic wrap and refrigerate at least 3 hours.

Invert terrine onto a cutting board. Remove plastic wrap and slice terrine ½-inch thick with a knife dipped in hot water for each cut.

# SALMON SHRIMP TERRINE

*A cross between a seafood mousse and a paté, this terrine is a sophisticated start to an elegant meal. Serve with* Beurre Blanc, *page 127.*

1/2 cup (1 stick) butter, softened, divided
1/4 cup chopped shallots or onion
8 oz. small shrimp, peeled and deveined
1 cup dry white wine
1 tbs. tomato paste
1 salmon fillet (10 oz.), boned and skinned

1 cup heavy cream
2 eggs
salt and pepper to taste
1 tbs. chopped fresh parsley
1 tbs. chopped fresh dill, or 1 tsp. dried

Heat oven to 300°. Melt 1/4 cup of the butter in a skillet over medium heat. Add shallots and cook for 2 minutes. Add shrimp and wine. Bring to a boil and stir in tomato paste; remove from heat. (The shrimp will not be fully cooked.) Set aside to cool slightly.

Cube salmon. Puree in a food processor workbowl along with remaining 1/4 cup butter, cream, eggs, salt, pepper, parsley and dill. Transfer to a bowl. Fold in cooled shrimp mixture. Spoon into a greased terrine or large loaf pan, smoothing the top with a spatula. Cover terrine. Place terrine in a larger pan, pour hot water in large pan to halfway up sides of terrine, and bake for 45 to 60 minutes. Remove terrine from water bath. Slice and serve warm.

# TERRINE OF SALMON

*Made a day or two in advance, this terrine is great served on a buffet.*

1 egg
2½ cups heavy cream, divided
4 slices white bread, crusts removed
1 medium onion, diced
¼ cup (½ stick) butter
1 salmon fillet (2½ lb.), boned and skinned

1 tsp. unflavored gelatin powder
salt and pepper to taste
¼ tsp. nutmeg
2 tbs. salmon caviar, optional, for garnish
½ bunch fresh dill, chopped
2 tbs. chopped fresh parsley

*Chum Salmon*

32   APPETIZERS AND HORS D'OEUVRES

Line a terrine or large loaf pan with plastic wrap. Heat oven to 375°.

In a small bowl, beat egg with ½ cup of the cream. Cube bread and add to cream mixture to soak 5 minutes. Meanwhile, in a small skillet over medium heat, sauté onion in butter until transparent.

Trim salmon fillet to fit terrine. Sprinkle trimmed fillet with gelatin powder and set aside.

Cube salmon trimmings and season with salt and pepper. Place salmon trimmings in a food processor workbowl. Add onion, bread with soaking liquid, salt and nutmeg. Process while slowly adding 1½ cups of the cream.

Fill prepared terrine ⅓ full with pureed mixture. Press trimmed salmon fillet in center. Top with remaining pureed salmon mixture, pressing to avoid air pockets. Enclose with plastic wrap. Cover with lid or foil. Place terrine in a larger baking pan. Pour hot water in larger pan to halfway up sides of terrine. Bake for 40 to 50 minutes. Remove from water bath and refrigerate terrine until cold.

Unmold terrine and roll terrine in herb mixture. Serve with remaining ½ cup cream, lightly beaten, and caviar, if using. Sprinkle with dill and parsley.

# SALMON-STUFFED EGGS

Makes 5 servings

*Deviled eggs go upscale with the addition of salmon and a cream sauce.*

| | |
|---|---|
| 2 tbs. butter | 5 eggs |
| 2 tbs. flour | 3 oz. cream cheese, softened |
| 2½ cups hot milk | 1 can (15 oz.) salmon, drained and flaked |
| salt and pepper to taste | 1 tbs. chopped fresh parsley |
| 1 tbs. tomato paste | 1 tbs. chopped fresh chives |

Heat oven to 350°. In a saucepan over medium heat, melt butter; mix in flour. Stir for 1 minute. Add milk and cook, stirring, until sauce thickens. Reduce heat to low and simmer for 5 minutes. Whisk in tomato paste. Keep warm.

Put eggs in a saucepan over high heat and cover with cold water. Bring to a simmer, reduce heat to low and simmer for 10 minutes. Remove eggs and dip in cold water. Remove shells and cut eggs in half lengthwise. Remove yolks and place in a bowl. Set aside egg white halves. Mash together egg yolks, cream cheese, ½ of the salmon, parsley, chives and 3 tbs. of the sauce. Fill egg whites with stuffing.

Stir remaining salmon into remaining sauce. Spread in a baking pan large enough to hold eggs. Arrange the stuffed eggs over sauce. Bake for 15 minutes until golden brown. Serve hot.

# SALADS AND PASTA

36  Smoked Salmon Spinach Salad
37  Smoked Salmon with Basil-Dressed Baby Greens
38  Grilled Salmon Salad
39  Salmon Salad
40  Creamed Fettuccine with Smoked Salmon
41  Fettuccine with Smoked Salmon Sauce
42  Cajun Salmon Fillet with Angel Hair Pasta
43  Fish Seasoning
44  Cold Salmon and Pasta
45  Pasta and Salmon Salad Suzanne
46  Summer Salmon Pasta

# SMOKED SALMON SPINACH SALAD

*This is a variation on a classic spinach salad. The savory hot dressing will wilt the spinach slightly. Serve this salad immediately.*

10 oz. fresh baby spinach
8 oz. cold-smoked salmon
8 slices Swiss cheese
$1/2$ cup olive oil
$1/4$ cup wine vinegar
1 tsp. honey
$1/4$ tsp. salt
$1/8$ tsp. pepper

Trim stems from spinach and shred leaves finely. Place in a large bowl. Cut smoked salmon and cheese into matchstick strips; set aside.

Place oil, vinegar, honey, salt and pepper in a saucepan over medium-high heat. Bring to a boil. Pour hot dressing over spinach and toss well.

Divide spinach among salad plates. Top with salmon and cheese.

# SMOKED SALMON
# WITH BASIL-DRESSED BABY GREENS

*Serve this bright and fresh salad with French bread as a first course or light lunch.*

1½ cups fresh basil
¼ cup olive oil
¼ cup water
⅓ cup white wine vinegar
3 cloves garlic, minced

½ tsp. salt
¼ tsp. pepper
1 lb. mixed baby greens
1 lb. cold-smoked salmon, thinly sliced

In a blender container, combine basil, olive oil, water, vinegar, garlic, salt and pepper. Puree until smooth. Transfer to a bowl. Cover and set aside.

Just before serving, toss greens with reserved dressing in a large bowl. Divide salad between plates. Roll slices of smoked salmon and arrange on top of salad.

# GRILLED SALMON SALAD

*Don't want to fire up the grill? Broil the salmon instead, with equally delicious results.*

1¼ cups olive oil, divided
6 tbs. lime juice
salt and pepper to taste
6 salmon fillets (8 oz. each)
3 small tomatoes, peeled, seeded and
   chopped
1 small carrot, cut into matchsticks
1 small zucchini, finely chopped

¼ cup chopped fresh parsley
¼ cup balsamic vinegar
3 tbs. pitted sliced green olives
1 tbs. minced fresh basil, or 1 tsp. dried
1 tbs. minced fresh tarragon, or 1 tsp. dried
1 tbs. capers
10 cups mixed baby greens

Mix ½ cup of the olive oil and lime juice in a small bowl. Season with salt and pepper. Place salmon in a glass or ceramic dish large enough to hold fillets in a single layer. Pour marinade over. Cover and refrigerate for 2 hours, turning once.

Combine tomatoes, carrot, zucchini, parsley, vinegar, remaining ¾ cup oil, olives, basil, tarragon and capers in a bowl. Season with salt and pepper; set aside. Prepare a medium-hot grill. Grill salmon until just cooked through, about 4 minutes per side. Discard marinade.

Toss greens with enough vegetable mixture to coat. Divide among 6 plates. Place salmon atop greens. Spoon additional vegetable mixture over and serve.

# SALMON SALAD

*Garnish the salad with tomato wedges and sliced cucumber for a refreshing hot-weather meal.*

½ cup mayonnaise
¼ cup prepared vinaigrette
salt and pepper to taste
1 lb. cooked salmon, boned, skinned and flaked

Combine mayonnaise, vinaigrette and salt and pepper in a small bowl. Place salmon in a medium bowl and fold in mayonnaise mixture. Refrigerate until serving.

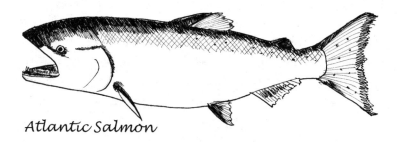

*Atlantic Salmon*

# CREAMED FETTUCCINE WITH SMOKED SALMON Makes 6 servings

*Fettuccine is made to accompany a rich sauce. This is an ideal luncheon dish.*

2 qt. chicken stock
2 tbs. butter
6 finely diced shallots, or ½ cup finely
    diced onion
3 cloves garlic, finely minced
4 oz. mushrooms, cut in matchsticks
1 cup dry white wine

½ jalapeño pepper, minced
1 cup heavy cream
salt and pepper to taste
3 medium tomatoes
1½ lb. fettuccine
½ cup chopped fresh basil
3 oz. cold-smoked salmon

Place chicken stock in a large saucepan over high heat and bring to a boil. While stock heats, in a large skillet over medium-high heat, melt butter. Add shallots, garlic and mushrooms. Cook, stirring, for 1 minute. Add wine. Boil to reduce by half. Stir in jalapeño and cream. Cook until reduced by half. Season with salt and pepper. Remove from heat. Peel and seed tomatoes. Cut into strips and stir into sauce. Keep sauce warm.

Cook pasta in the boiling chicken stock. Drain pasta (do not rinse). Just before serving, cut basil and salmon into thin strips. Gently toss pasta with salmon and basil. Serve with sauce.

# FETTUCCINE WITH SMOKED SALMON SAUCE

*An ideal tasty recipe served as a light lunch. Some of the smoked salmon is used to make the sauce.*

1 tbs. shallots or onions, chopped
1/2 cup dry white wine
1 1/2 cups half-and-half
6 oz. cold-smoked salmon, sliced
salt and pepper to taste

1/8 tsp. cayenne pepper
8 oz. fettuccine
1 cup peas
2 tbs. olive oil
1 tbs. chopped fresh parsley

In a non-aluminum saucepan over medium-high heat, combine shallots and wine. Boil until liquid is almost evaporated. Add half-and-half, reduce heat to low and simmer for 5 minutes. Pour sauce in a blender container. Cut smoked salmon into strips. Add 1/2 of the salmon to sauce and puree until smooth. Pour sauce back into saucepan. Season with salt, pepper and cayenne. Keep warm.

Cook fettuccine in salted boiling water, adding peas during the last minute of cooking. Drain fettuccini and peas and toss with olive oil. Arrange pasta and peas on plates. Sprinkle smoked salmon strips over. Pour warm sauce over pasta and sprinkle with parsley. Serve immediately.

# CAJUN SALMON FILLET
# WITH ANGEL HAIR PASTA

Makes 6 servings

*The marinated salmon fillet is balanced by the delicate pasta.*

1 salmon fillet (2 lb.)
1 tbs. Worcestershire sauce
1/2 tsp. onion salt
1 tsp. *Fish Seasoning*, page 43
1 tsp. dried oregano

2 tbs. capers
8 oz. angel hair pasta
1/4 cup (1/2 stick) butter
*Beurre Blanc*, page 127

Heat oven to 450°. Butter a baking pan large enough for the salmon fillet. Remove bones from fillet and place skin side down in baking pan. Season with Worcestershire, onion salt, *Fish Seasoning* and oregano. Bake salmon for 10 minutes. Turn on broiler and broil salmon for 2 to 3 minutes to brown the top. Sprinkle capers over fish.

While salmon is baking, cook pasta in salted boiling water. Drain pasta and toss with butter. Keep warm.

Divide salmon fillet into 6 equal portions. Arrange each portion on a hot plate. Drizzle with liquid from the baking pan, then with hot pasta. Serve with *Beurre Blanc.*

# FISH SEASONING

*This Cajun-style seasoning blend will enhance your grilled and baked salmon recipes. This recipe can be doubled, and will keep for months.*

1 tbs. sweet paprika
1 tsp. salt
1 tsp. onion powder
1 tsp. cayenne pepper
1 tsp. garlic powder
$1/2$ tsp. ground white pepper
$1/2$ tsp. ground black pepper
$1/2$ tsp. dried thyme
$1/2$ tsp. dried oregano

Blend all ingredients together. Seal in an airtight container and store in a dry place away from heat.

# COLD SALMON AND PASTA

*This dish is colorful with subtle flavors and texture.*

8 oz. small shell-shaped pasta
8 oz. cooked salmon, boned and skinned
3 medium carrots
1 bunch watercress
1/2 cup olive oil
1/4 cup lemon juice

1 tbs. Dijon mustard
1 clove garlic, minced
1 tsp. dried tarragon
salt and pepper to taste
1 cup Italian black olives, pitted
2 tbs. capers, rinsed

Cook pasta in salted boiling water, drain, run under cold water and drain again. Set aside. Flake salmon. (If canned, drain, remove skin and bones and flake.) Set aside.

Slice carrots into 1/4-inch rounds. Cook in salted boiling water in a saucepan for 10 minutes. Drain. Remove coarse stems from watercress.

In a large bowl, whisk together oil, lemon juice, mustard, garlic, tarragon, salt and pepper. Add the reserved pasta, salmon, carrots, watercress, olives and capers. Toss to combine and refrigerate before serving.

# PASTA AND SALMON SALAD SUZANNE

*This colorful cold pasta salad is easy to prepare and can be made a day ahead. Serve on lettuce leaves with a basket of crusty bread.*

12 oz. macaroni or other small pasta
½ lb. broccoli
1 cup mayonnaise
2 tbs. tomato sauce
1 can (8 oz.) salmon

1 red bell pepper, thinly sliced
½ cup grated Parmesan cheese
¼ cup shredded fresh basil
salt and pepper to taste

Cook pasta in boiling salted water, drain, rinse under cold water and drain again.

Cut broccoli into bite-sized florets. Cook in salted boiling water for 2 minutes. Drain immediately and rinse under cold water to stop the cooking and keep broccoli green.

In a small bowl, stir together mayonnaise and tomato sauce; set aside. Drain salmon and separate into chunks.

In a large bowl, combine pasta, salmon, bell pepper, broccoli, Parmesan, basil, salt and pepper. Stir in dressing. Season to taste. Refrigerate for at least 1 hour. Toss salad again just before serving.

# SUMMER SALMON PASTA

*Use canned salmon, drained, if you don't have leftover cooked salmon.*

8 oz. small shell pasta
1 large seedless cucumber
8 oz. cooked salmon, boned and skinned
1 1/2 cups mayonnaise
1 tbs. chopped scallion
1 tsp. fresh dill, or 1/2 tsp. dried

1 tbs. vinegar
salt and pepper to taste
2 cups shredded iceberg lettuce
1/2 cup pitted, halved ripe olives
2 cups halved cherry tomatoes
1 cup peas

Cook pasta in boiling salted water, drain, rinse under cold water and drain again. Set aside.

Peel cucumber, cut in half lengthwise, remove seeds and slice across. Flake salmon. (If canned, drain and remove skin and bones, then flake.)

In a bowl, whisk together mayonnaise, scallion, dill, vinegar, salt and pepper.

In a large glass bowl, layer lettuce, pasta, olives, tomatoes, cucumbers, peas and salmon. Pour 3/4 cup of the dressing over the top. Refrigerate at least 1 hour. Toss salad at the table and pass remaining dressing.

# ENTRÉES

49  Kedgeree of Salmon
50  Smoked Salmon Omelet
51  Smoked Salmon Pizza
52  Smoked Salmon Crêpes
53  Smoked Salmon Croque Monsieur
54  Smoked Salmon Soufflé
55  Pan-Smoked Salmon
56  Salmon Croquettes with Butter Sauce
58  Brochettes of Salmon
59  Gougeonnettes of Salmon
60  Salmon Burgers
61  Salmon Cakes
62  Salmon and Corn Chowder
63  Baked Salmon Fillets
64  Salmon Fillets with Basil Sauce
65  Broiled Fillets of Salmon with Ginger Cream
66  Fillets of Salmon in Potato Crust
68  Salmon Fillets in a Horseradish-Ginger Crust
69  Salmon with Mustard-Honey Crust
70  Salmon with Roasted Garlic
71  Grilled Mustard-Dill Salmon Fillet
72  Grilled Asian Salmon with Japanese Eggplant
73  Honey-Lime Salmon Fillets
74  Pine Nut-Crusted Salmon
75  Poached Salmon with Watercress Mayonnaise
76  Phyllo-Wrapped Salmon
77  Salmon Bonne Femme
78  Salmon en Croûte
79  Salmon in Red Wine Sauce
80  Salmon Teriyaki
81  Salmon with Riesling-Caper Sauce
82  Seared Salmon with Thai Vegetables
83  Thai Vegetables

| 84 | Salmon Fillets with Mustard-Horseradish Vinaigrette |
|----|----|
| 85 | Stuffed Salmon Fillet |
| 86 | Salmon Steaks with Apricot-Horseradish Sauce |
| 87 | Salmon with Ginger Ratatouille |
| 88 | Braised Salmon Steaks with Fennel |
| 89 | Broiled Pacific Salmon Steaks with Salsa Butter |
| 90 | Cold Poached Salmon Steaks |
| 91 | Salmon Steaks in White Wine Sauce |
| 92 | Poached Salmon Steaks with Mustard-Parsley Sauce |
| 94 | Salmon Steaks en Papillote |
| 95 | Salmon Steaks Italienne |
| 96 | Salmon Steaks in Champagne Sauce |
| 97 | Salmon Tortillas |
| 98 | Salmon Roast with Lentils |
| 100 | Baked Whole Salmon |
| 102 | Braised Blueback Salmon with White Wine Sauce |
| 104 | Grilled Whole Salmon with Lemon-Rice Stuffing |
| 106 | Tournedos of Salmon |
| 107 | Steelhead Napa Valley |
| 108 | Whole Roasted Salmon with Wild Rice Stuffing |
| 110 | Whole Salmon with Cream Sauce |
| 112 | Matelote of Salmon |
| 114 | Salmon and Wild Rice Pie |
| 116 | Creamed Salmon Casserole |
| 117 | Salmon Cutlets Pojarsky |
| 118 | Salmon-in-a-Crust |
| 120 | Salmon Florentine |
| 121 | Salmon Provençale |

# KEDGEREE OF SALMON

Serves: 8

*This colorful dish uses fresh and smoked salmon, decorated in yellow, white and green.*

1 tbs. butter
3 medium chopped scallions
1 cup sour cream
1½ tbs. curry powder
1 lb. salmon, poached, skinned and boned
½ lb. smoked salmon, diced
1 cup converted rice

2 cups chicken broth
2 hard cooked eggs
1 tbs. onion, chopped
1 tbs. soft butter
2 tbs. parsley, chopped
8 sprigs fresh parsley
1 cup lemon butter with Dijon mustard

Preheat oven to 400°. Melt butter in a sauté pan. Cook scallions over low heat for 5 minutes. Add sour cream and curry powder and mix well. Flake cooked salmon. Combine with smoked salmon. In a separate pot, stir rice with chicken broth. Bring to a boil. Cover and cook over medium heat until liquid is almost absorbed. Separate egg yolks from whites. Chop egg whites and reserve. Chop egg yolks and save for garnish. Combine rice and salmon mixture. Add egg whites. Butter a deep casserole dish and spoon salmon-rice mixture into dish. Bake at 400° for 10 minutes. Lower oven temperature to 350° and bake for 40 to 45 minutes.

To serve, unmold kedgeree unto a serving platter. Garnish top with rows of chopped egg yolks, onion and parsley. Garnish platter with sprigs of parsley. Serve with lemon butter.

# SMOKED SALMON OMELET

*Serve this omelet with buttered toast or bagels, or add a salad for a fast, light lunch.*

4 eggs
1 tbs. chopped fresh dill, or 1 tsp. dried
1 tsp. vegetable oil
1 scallion, finely chopped
4 oz. smoked salmon (hot- or cold-smoked), chopped
2 oz. cream cheese, cut into thin strips

In a small bowl, beat eggs with dill for about a minute. Heat oil in a skillet over medium heat. Cook scallion for a minute or so, until aroma is released. Pour eggs into hot skillet and cook, lifting edges with a spatula several times to allow uncooked egg to run to the bottom of skillet. When bottom of omelet is firm, flip gently with a spatula. Sprinkle smoked salmon on half of the omelet, and top with strips of cream cheese.

Fold the other half-circle over the top of the half with the filling, cover skillet with a lid, and cook for a minute over low heat. Serve immediately.

# SMOKED SALMON PIZZA

*Serve this pizza also as hors d'oeuvres, cut into small pieces. Mascarpone is a smooth Italian cream cheese. Bake the pizzas on a cookie sheet if you don't have a pizza stone.*

$3/4$ cup mascarpone cheese or cream cheese
2 medium shallots, minced, or $1/4$ cup minced onion
1 tbs. lemon juice
2 tbs. chopped fresh chives, divided
salt and pepper to taste
2 baked pizza crusts (10- to12-inch)
6 oz. cold-smoked salmon, chopped

Put a pizza stone on the lowest rack of a cold oven. Heat oven to 400°.

In a small bowl, mix cheese, shallots, lemon juice and 1 tbs. of the chives. Season with salt and pepper. Spread over pizza crusts. Slide pizzas onto the pizza stone. Bake 15 minutes, or until crust is golden brown. Immediately sprinkle with salmon and remaining 1 tbs. chives. Serve hot.

# SMOKED SALMON CRÊPES

*The crêpes can be made a day ahead, stacked (without fillings), covered in plastic wrap, and refrigerated. Serve the filled crêpes with a green salad.*

½ cup flour
¼ tsp. salt
2 eggs
¾ cup milk

3 tbs. melted butter, cooled
½ lb. thinly sliced cold-smoked salmon
1 cup crème fraîche or sour cream
salt and pepper to taste

In a medium bowl, combine flour, salt, eggs and milk and whisk until smooth. Whisk in butter. Set aside to rest for 30 minutes at room temperature.

Place a small nonstick skillet over medium heat. Pour in ¼ cup batter, tilting skillet to coat bottom of pan. Cook crêpe until golden brown on the bottom. Flip crêpe and cook other side for 30 seconds. Transfer to a plate and cover with a sheet of parchment paper or foil. Repeat until all crêpe batter is used.

Heat broiler. Butter a baking pan. Cut salmon into 2-inch-long strips, about ¼-inch wide. Divide salmon strips among the crêpes, forming a line down the center of each. Roll crêpes into cylinders and arrange seam side down in the prepared dish. Season crème fraîche with salt and pepper and spoon ½ cup over crêpes. Broil until top is golden brown, about 5 minutes. Serve, passing remaining crème fraîche separately.

# SMOKED SALMON CROQUE MONSIEUR

Makes 6 servings

*This translation of the French ham-and-cheese sandwich loses nothing in the way of richness. Serve these for lunch, or cut into small squares for hot hors d'oeuvres.*

$\frac{1}{2}$ cup (1 stick) butter, softened, divided (or more as needed)
1 sweet onion (Vidalia, Maui or Walla Walla), finely chopped
12 slices brioche or country-style white bread
12 thin slices Fontina cheese
$\frac{1}{2}$ lb. sliced cold-smoked salmon

In a small skillet, melt 2 tbs. of the butter over low heat. Add onion and cook until soft and translucent, about 10 minutes. Set aside.

Spread 1 side of each bread slice with 1 tsp. of the butter. Place a slice of fontina on each piece of bread. Top with onion, dividing evenly.

Heat oven to 200°. In a large nonstick skillet, melt remaining 2 tbs. butter over low heat. Working in batches, place bread slices, cheese side up, in skillet and heat until cheese is melted and bread is golden underneath, adding more butter to skillet as needed. As each batch is done, place on a baking sheet and keep warm in the oven. Place 6 of the slices on a cutting board and cover them with smoked salmon. Top with remaining slices, cheese sides down. Cut on the diagonal and serve.

# SMOKED SALMON SOUFFLÉ

*The trick to making an easy, light soufflé: Fold the beaten egg whites gently into the base sauce, and don't open the oven door while the soufflé is cooking.*

6 tbs. ($^3/_4$ stick) butter, divided
1 tbs. minced shallots or onion
$^1/_2$ cup dry white wine
$^1/_4$ cup flour
$1^1/_2$ cups hot milk
$^1/_4$ tsp. pepper
$^1/_8$ tsp. nutmeg

4 oz. mushrooms, diced
8 oz. smoked salmon (hot- or cold-smoked), chopped
5 egg yolks
5 egg whites
$^1/_4$ tsp. cream of tartar

Heat oven to 350°. Butter and flour a 7-inch soufflé dish; set aside. Melt $^1/_4$ cup of the butter in a non-aluminum saucepan over medium heat. Add shallots and wine and cook until wine is almost evaporated. Stir in flour and cook for 5 minutes. Whisk in milk and cook until sauce thickens and comes to a boil. Season with pepper and nutmeg. Set aside to cool.

In a skillet over medium heat sauté mushrooms in remaining 2 tbs. butter for 3 minutes. Cool for 5 minutes and mix in salmon. Whisk egg yolks into sauce, then stir in mushroom-salmon mixture. In a bowl, beat egg whites until stiff peaks form. Fold into salmon mixture. Spoon soufflé batter into prepared dish. Bake 30 minutes. Serve immediately.

# PAN-SMOKED SALMON

*This is a homemade hot-smoked salmon that gives great results. A cast-iron skillet is necessary, as it can take the high heat required. You may want to open a window for ventilation.*

2 tsp. sugar
1 tsp. salt
1 tsp. pepper

4 salmon fillets (4 oz. each)
1 tbs. wood chips
1 tsp. olive oil

In a small bowl, combine sugar, salt and pepper. Place salmon fillets in a shallow dish and sprinkle sugar mixture over each fillet. Turn fillets over. Cover dish with plastic wrap, and refrigerate for 1 to 3 hours.

Line a 10- or 11-inch cast-iron skillet with aluminum foil. Cut a 2-inch hole in the center where the wood chips will be placed in direct contact with the bottom of the skillet. Heat skillet over high heat until very hot, 3 to 5 minutes. Line a heavy lid to fit the skillet with foil. Brush salmon fillets with olive oil. Arrange wood chips in the center of the hot pan. Place a wire rack with 1-inch-high feet in skillet. Arrange salmon fillets on rack. Cover tightly and reduce heat to medium. Smoke salmon fillets for about 10 minutes. Test inside of fillets for doneness. Serve at once or refrigerate and serve cold.

# SALMON CROQUETTES WITH BUTTER SAUCE

Makes 6 servings

*Freshly poached salmon or leftovers are made into elegant croquettes. The lemon-chive-butter sauce adds richness.*

1 cup (2 sticks) butter, divided
$1/3$ cup plus $3/4$ cup flour, divided
1 cup hot milk
salt and pepper to taste
2 egg yolks
1 lb. cooked salmon fillet, boned and
   skinned
1 tbs. lemon juice

3 tbs. chopped fresh chives
2 eggs
2 tbs. water
2 cups fresh breadcrumbs
$1/4$ tsp. salt
$1/8$ tsp. pepper
oil for deep-frying

Melt $1/4$ cup of the butter in a medium saucepan over low heat. Add $1/3$ cup of the flour and cook, whisking, for about 3 minutes. Whisk in milk, raise heat to medium and bring to a boil, whisking constantly. Season with salt and pepper. Reduce heat to low. Whisk a few tbs. of the hot sauce into egg yolks in a small bowl. Stir egg yolk mixture back into sauce in the saucepan. Heat sauce, stirring, for 2 minutes longer, until very thick and smooth. Flake salmon and fold into sauce.

Transfer salmon mixture to a bowl, cover with plastic wrap and refrigerate until cold.

Melt remaining ¾ cup butter in a saucepan over low heat. Skim foam from surface. Remove saucepan from heat and set aside for a few minutes until milk solids settle to the bottom. Pour the clear butter into another saucepan, discarding solids in the bottom of the pan. Whisk lemon juice into clarified butter. Add chives and season with salt and pepper. Keep sauce warm.

Shape cold salmon mixture into 12 pear-shaped croquettes. Place remaining ¾ cup flour in a shallow bowl. Beat eggs with water in a second shallow bowl. Place breadcrumbs in a third shallow bowl; season with salt and pepper. Dredge croquettes in flour, dip in beaten eggs and roll in breadcrumbs to coat well. Set aside.

Place oil in a large deep skillet to a depth of 1 to 1½ inches. Place over medium-high heat and heat oil to 350° on a thermometer. Deep-fry croquettes, a few at a time, in hot oil for 3 minutes or until golden brown. Drain on paper towels.

Arrange 2 croquettes on each plate. Serve butter-lemon sauce separately.

# BROCHETTES OF SALMON

*To serve these kabobs as appetizers, thread one cube of salmon and one mushroom cap on each skewer.*

1 salmon fillet (2¹/₂ lb.)
salt and pepper to taste
1 tbs. lemon juice, divided
24 mushroom caps

¹/₂ cup (1 stick) butter, divided
2 oz. fresh breadcrumbs
2 tbs. vegetable oil

Bone and skin salmon. Cut into 1-inch cubes. Season with salt, pepper and 2 tsp. of the lemon juice; set aside. Sprinkle mushrooms with remaining 1 tsp. lemon juice.

Sauté mushroom caps in ¹/₄ cup of the butter over medium heat in a large skillet for 2 minutes on each side. Thread salmon pieces and mushroom caps alternately on metal or bamboo skewers. Dip brochettes in remaining ¹/₄ cup melted butter and roll in breadcrumbs.

Heat oil in the same skillet over medium-high heat. Cook salmon brochettes until evenly golden brown, about 10 minutes.

# GOUGEONNETTES OF SALMON

Makes 6 servings

*These crisp little strips of fried salmon are delicious with* Tartar Sauce, *page 147.*

2 lb. salmon fillets, boned and skinned
1/2 tsp. salt
1/4 tsp. pepper
1 tbs. lemon juice
1 cup flour

4 eggs, beaten
2 cups fresh breadcrumbs
oil for frying
6 lemon wedges, for garnish
1 cup chopped fresh parsley, for garnish

Cut salmon into strips about 4 x 2 inches. Season with salt, pepper and lemon juice. Place flour in a shallow bowl, eggs in a second shallow bowl, and breadcrumbs in a third shallow bowl. Dredge salmon strips in flour, dip in beaten eggs and roll in breadcrumbs to coat well. In a large deep skillet, pour oil to a depth of at least 1 inch and place over medium-high heat. Heat oil to 350° on an instant-read thermometer. Deep-fry the breaded salmon for 2 to 3 minutes, or until golden brown.

Garnish gougeonnettes with lemon wedges and parsley.

# SALMON BURGERS

*These salmon patties are served on hamburger buns and can be served with tomatoes and lettuce if desired. In contrast with beef burgers, salmon burgers are very low in saturated fat.*

1½ lb. cooked salmon
½ cup dry breadcrumbs
¼ cup chopped onions
½ cup chopped celery
½ cup mayonnaise

1 egg
salt and pepper to taste
1 tbs. canola oil
6 hamburger-type buns, split and toasted

Skin, bone and flake salmon into a bowl. Add breadcrumbs, onion and celery. Mix well. In a small bowl, combine mayonnaise, egg, salt and pepper. Stir egg mixture gently into salmon mixture until well combined. Refrigerate until ready to use.

Shape salmon mixture into 6 patties about 1-inch thick. Heat oil in a nonstick skillet over medium heat. Place patties in the pan. Cook until browned on both sides. Place on warm toasted buns. Garnish as desired.

# SALMON CAKES

*Lovely on their own, these salmon cakes are spectacular with* Cream Sauce with Chives, *page 134, or* Cucumber Paprika Sauce, *page 135.*

1½ lb. cooked salmon, boned and skinned
2 eggs, beaten
1¼ cups cracker crumbs or breadcrumbs,
    divided
½ tsp. paprika

¼ cup chopped fresh chives
2 tbs. chopped fresh parsley
salt and pepper to taste
2 tbs. oil (or more as needed)
6 lemon wedges, for garnish

Flake salmon into a bowl with eggs, ½ cup of the crumbs, paprika, chives and parsley. Stir gently until well combined. Season with salt and pepper. Shape mixture into 12 cakes. Place remaining ¾ cup crumbs in a shallow bowl; coat cakes on all sides with crumbs.

Heat oil in a large skillet over medium heat. Add a few cakes at a time and cook 3 minutes on each side or until golden brown. Drain on paper towels and keep warm while cooking remaining cakes, adding more oil if necessary. Serve hot with lemon wedges.

# SALMON AND CORN CHOWDER

*This is a simple version of the classic corn chowder. Add the salmon to the simmering chowder a few minutes before serving, as it cooks quickly.*

2 tbs. butter
1 medium carrot, diced
1 small onion, chopped
1 leek, cleaned and sliced
1 medium potato, peeled and cubed
2 cups milk
1 cup chicken or vegetable stock

salt and pepper to taste
1 cup corn
6 oz. salmon fillet, boned, skinned and cubed
1/2 cup heavy cream
1 tbs. chopped fresh parsley

Melt butter in a large saucepan over medium heat. Add carrot and cook for 2 minutes. Add onion and leek and cook, stirring occasionally, until transparent. Stir in potato and cook for 1 minute; pour in milk and stock. Season well with salt and pepper, reduce heat to low and simmer gently for 10 minutes. Add corn and salmon and simmer 3 to 4 minutes longer, until salmon and potatoes are cooked through. Stir in cream and parsley. Heat and serve immediately.

# BAKED SALMON FILLETS

*Mustard-chive-lemon butter is the perfect topping for this simple dish and will enhance the fine flavor of the salmon.*

5 tbs. butter, softened
2 tbs. lemon juice, divided
1½ tbs. chopped fresh chives
2 tsp. grainy Dijon mustard
1 tsp. grated lemon zest
salt and pepper to taste
4 salmon fillets (6 oz. each)

Heat oven to 400°. In a small bowl, mix butter, 2 tsp. of the lemon juice, chives, mustard, lemon zest, salt and pepper until well blended. Line a baking pan with foil. Rub 1 tbs. of the mustard-chive butter over foil. Place fillets skin side down on foil and spoon about 1 tsp. remaining lemon juice on each fillet. Season with salt and pepper. Top each fillet with 1 tbs. mustard-chive butter. Bake for 12 to 15 minutes.

Spoon chive-butter sauce from the baking pan over salmon. Serve hot.

# SALMON FILLETS WITH BASIL SAUCE

*A classic, delicious recipe with a twist: basil adds an herbal note to a basic cream sauce.*

6 salmon fillets (5 oz. each), boned and skinned
salt and pepper to taste
3 tbs. olive oil
1 tbs. chopped shallots or onion
1 tsp. minced garlic
2 cups fresh basil leaves
$\frac{1}{2}$ cup dry white wine
$\frac{1}{2}$ cup heavy cream

Season salmon fillets with salt and pepper. Heat oil in a skillet over medium-high heat until hot. Brown salmon fillets on 1 side for about 3 minutes. Turn salmon. Reduce heat to medium and cook salmon for 3 to 5 minutes, or until just cooked through. Transfer salmon to a platter and keep warm. Add shallots and garlic to the pan. Cook over medium heat for 1 minute; do not brown. Add basil leaves and wine to the pan. Simmer to wilt basil. Stir cream into sauce. Simmer until sauce is reduced by half. Season to taste. Spoon sauce over hot salmon.

# BROILED FILLETS OF SALMON
# WITH GINGER CREAM

*The broiled salmon fillets are served with a creamy and tangy ginger sauce. Salmon steaks can also be used with this recipe.*

2 cups *Fish Fumet*, page 126
1 cup dry white wine
2 tbs. chopped shallots or onion
1 cup heavy cream

2 tbs. grated fresh ginger
¼ cup (½ stick) butter
6 salmon fillets (6 oz. each), with skin
salt and pepper to taste

In a non-aluminum saucepan over medium-high heat, combine *Fish Fumet*, wine and shallots. Bring to a boil and cook until liquid is reduced by half. Add cream and ginger. Return to a boil. Reduce again by half or until lightly thickened. Pour sauce through a strainer. Whisk in butter, a few bits at a time. Set sauce aside and keep warm.

Heat broiler. Arrange salmon fillets skin side up in an oiled baking pan. Season with salt and pepper. Place salmon under the broiler, 4 inches from the source of heat. Broil for 10 to 12 minutes until skin is crisp and flesh is opaque. Serve with warm sauce.

# FILLETS OF SALMON IN POTATO CRUST

*The salmon fillets are wrapped in paper-thin, scale-like potato slices. A rich red wine sauce transforms this dish into a unique creation.*

4 salmon fillets (7 oz. each), boned and skinned
salt and pepper to taste
1 tsp. chopped fresh thyme, or ½ tsp. dried
2 extra-large baking potatoes, peeled
2 tbs. butter, or more as needed
2 tbs. vegetable oil, or more as needed
1 tbs. minced fresh chives, for garnish
*Red Wine Sauce,* page 137

Heat oven to 450°. Make each fillet rectangular (about 5 x 2 inches) by trimming off the uneven edges with a sharp knife. Season fillets with salt and pepper and sprinkle them with thyme.

Cut ½ of 1 potato lengthwise into paper-thin, long slices with a vegetable peeler or on a mandoline. Do not rinse the potato slices as the starch will help the wrapped slices stick together. Place potato slices on a work surface, overlapping slices until they can be wrapped all around 1 fillet. Season potato with salt. Center a salmon fillet in the middle of the potato slices. Fold the edges of potatoes over salmon to enclose it entirely. (Since the potato slices are not washed, starch discolors the potato rapidly. To avoid any discoloration, cook the fillets 1 at a time as soon as they are wrapped.).

Melt butter and oil in a nonstick skillet over high heat. Add wrapped fillet with potato seam side down and sauté until golden brown, 3 to 5 minutes on each side. While the first fillet is cooking, slice enough potato to wrap another fillet. Cook as soon as it is made. Continue with the remaining potatoes and salmon fillets, adding more butter and oil to the skillet if necessary. Transfer the browned, wrapped fillets to a baking sheet.

Just before serving, place all 4 potato-wrapped fillets in the oven for 5 minutes. Meanwhile, warm *Red Wine Sauce* in a small saucepan over low heat.

Drizzle fillets of salmon with a little sauce. Garnish with minced chives. Serve remaining sauce separately.

# SALMON FILLETS IN A HORSERADISH-GINGER CRUST

*As fast as it is delicious, this salmon takes no time to prepare.*

4 salmon fillets (5 oz. each), boned and skinned
1¼ cups fresh breadcrumbs
¼ cup grated horseradish, squeezed dry
1 tbs. grated fresh ginger

1 tbs. canola or vegetable oil
3 tbs. rice wine, divided
salt and pepper to taste
2 tbs. soy sauce
2 tbs. water

Heat broiler. Lightly oil a baking sheet. Set salmon on the baking sheet.

In a food processor workbowl, combine breadcrumbs, horseradish, ginger, oil, 1 tbs. of the rice wine, salt and pepper. Process until well blended and moist. Press ¼ of the crumb mixture over top of each salmon fillet. Broil about 4 inches from the heat source, until crust is golden brown and salmon is opaque in the center, about 8 to 10 minutes.

While salmon is broiling, stir soy sauce, remaining 2 tbs. rice wine and water in a small bowl. Serve alongside the salmon.

# SALMON WITH MUSTARD-HONEY CRUST

*Garnish with thinly sliced deep-fried leeks — a gourmet twist on fried onions.*

1/4 cup grainy mustard
2 tbs. honey
2 tsp. balsamic vinegar
4 salmon fillets (7 oz. each), boned and
 skinned
1 cup boiling water
1 cup couscous

2 tsp. butter
salt and pepper to taste
2 cups diced pineapple
1 tbs. chopped fresh tarragon, or 1 tsp. dried
1 clove garlic, chopped
2 tsp. raspberry vinegar

Heat oven to 400°. In a small bowl, combine mustard, honey and vinegar. Place salmon on a baking sheet and brush with mustard mixture. Bake for about 10 minutes, or until just cooked through.

While salmon bakes, pour boiling water over the couscous in a bowl. Set aside for 10 minutes. Stir in butter, salt and pepper. Fluff couscous with a fork and keep warm.

In a separate bowl, combine pineapple, tarragon, garlic, raspberry vinegar, salt and pepper. Garnish salmon with hot couscous and pineapple relish. Serve hot.

# SALMON WITH ROASTED GARLIC

*Roasted garlic is sweet and mellow, and will enhance rather than overpower the salmon.*

2 medium bulbs garlic
1/2 cup olive oil, about
3 tbs. butter, softened
8 salmon fillets (6 oz. each)

4 tsp. lemon juice
4 tsp. chopped fresh rosemary, or 1 tsp.
   dried

Heat oven to 400°. Slice top off garlic bulbs and place in an ovenproof dish just large enough to hold them. Pour in enough oil to cover. Wrap in a double layer of foil. Bake until very tender, about 35 minutes. Using a slotted spoon, transfer garlic to a work surface; reserve oil. Squeeze softened garlic out of the papery skins. Place garlic and oil in a food processor workbowl. Add butter and puree. Season with salt and pepper.

Heat oven to 450°. Arrange salmon fillets on a baking sheet. Season with salt and pepper. Sprinkle with lemon juice and spread 1 tbs. of garlic butter over each.

Bake, uncovered, for about 15 minutes, until salmon is just cooked through. Sprinkle with rosemary. Spoon remaining garlic butter over each fillet. Serve hot.

# GRILLED MUSTARD-DILL SALMON FILLET

*Grilling the salmon outdoors is a recipe for a relaxing time. The light and tangy sauce balances the richness of the fish.*

| | |
|---|---|
| 1/4 cup lemon juice | pepper to taste |
| 1/4 cup Dijon mustard | 1 salmon fillet (2 lb.), skin on |
| 1/4 cup olive oil | 1 cup plain yogurt |
| 3 tbs. minced shallots or onion | 1 tbs. grated lemon zest |
| 1/2 cup chopped fresh dill | dill sprigs, for garnish |

In a shallow glass or ceramic dish just large enough to hold fish, whisk together lemon juice, mustard, oil, shallots, dill and pepper. Add salmon fillet and turn to coat both sides. Cover. Refrigerate for 30 minutes, or up to 3 hours. Bring to room temperature before grilling.

In a small bowl, combine yogurt and lemon zest. Refrigerate until serving time.

Prepare a medium fire in a covered grill; oil grill rack. Place salmon fillet, skin side down, on rack. Cover grill and cook until salmon is well browned on bottom, about 10 minutes. Carefully turn over, using 2 wide spatulas. Grill, covered, until salmon is just opaque, 8 to 10 minutes longer. Transfer salmon fillet skin side down to a platter. Garnish with fresh dill sprigs. Serve with reserved yogurt-lemon sauce.

# GRILLED ASIAN SALMON
# WITH JAPANESE EGGPLANT

Makes 6 servings

*Japanese eggplants are smaller and more delicate than their American cousins. If you can't find Japanese eggplant, use one large American eggplant instead, sliced 1-inch thick.*

6 salmon steaks or fillets (6 oz. each)
3 Japanese eggplants, halved lengthwise
1/2 cup hoisin sauce
2 tbs. red wine

2 tbs. orange juice
1 tbs. soy sauce
1 tbs. minced fresh ginger
1/2 tsp. Chinese chili sauce

Place salmon in a glass dish in 1 layer; place eggplants in a second glass dish. Combine hoisin sauce, wine, orange juice, ginger and chili sauce in a small bowl; pour 1/2 over salmon and 1/2 over eggplants. Marinate salmon and eggplants for 30 minutes.

While they are marinating, prepare a hot fire on a grill. Reserve marinade from eggplants; discard salmon marinade. Grill eggplants and salmon for 3 to 4 minutes per side, until salmon is cooked through and eggplant is tender. Baste with reserved marinade on both sides while grilling.

# HONEY-LIME SALMON FILLETS

*This is a quick recipe full of flavor. Serve with* Black Bean and Mango Salsa, *page 149.*

4 large shallots, minced, or 1/3 cup minced onion
2 large cloves garlic, minced
1/2 jalapeño pepper, minced
juice from 3 limes
3 tbs. honey
3 tbs. olive oil
6 salmon fillets (5 oz. each), boned and skinned

In a small bowl, combine shallots, garlic and jalapeño. Add lime juice and honey. Set aside.

Heat oil in a large skillet over medium-high heat until hot. Sauté salmon fillets on 1 side for about 3 minutes. Flip salmon and add shallot mixture. Reduce heat to medium and cook salmon for 3 to 5 minutes or until cooked through.

Arrange each salmon fillet on a hot plate. Spoon honey-lime sauce over.

# PINE NUT-CRUSTED SALMON

Makes 4 servings

*This recipe gives salmon a nutty flavor. Served with lemon sauce, it is delicious.*

1/4 cup fresh breadcrumbs
1/2 cup pine nuts (pignoli)
4 salmon fillets (6 oz. each)
1 1/2 tbs. Dijon mustard
1 tsp. vegetable oil

5 tbs. cold butter, divided
2 tbs. lemon juice
1/4 cup heavy cream
salt and pepper to taste

Heat oven to 350°. Spread breadcrumbs and pine nuts on a cookie sheet and bake for 10 minutes, stirring once, until golden. Leave oven at 350°.

Brush salmon with mustard. Sprinkle breadcrumb mixture over salmon, pressing to adhere to the fish. Heat oil and 1 tbs. of the butter in an ovenproof skillet over medium heat. Add salmon crumb side down and cook until golden brown, about 3 to 5 minutes. Gently turn fish over. Transfer skillet to oven. Bake for 8 to 10 minutes, until cooked through.

While salmon is baking, in a small non-aluminum saucepan over medium-high heat, boil lemon juice until reduced to 1 tsp. Add cream and boil until slightly thickened. Whisk in remaining 1/4 cup butter a bit at a time until sauce is smooth. Season with salt and pepper. Spoon sauce around fish. Serve hot.

# POACHED SALMON
# WITH WATERCRESS MAYONNAISE

*Classic cold poached salmon, served with a tangy green mayonnaise, is ideal on a hot summer day.*

3/4 cup mayonnaise
1/2 cup finely chopped watercress
1 tbs. coarse-grained Dijon mustard
1 tsp. lemon juice
salt and pepper to taste
1/3 cup water

1/3 cup dry white wine
1 shallot, thinly sliced, or 2 tbs. minced onion
2 tbs. chopped fresh parsley
1 fresh thyme sprig
6 salmon fillets (6 oz. each) with skin

Blend mayonnaise, watercress, mustard and lemon juice in a small bowl; season with salt and pepper. Refrigerate until ready to use.

Combine water, wine, shallot, parsley and thyme in large skillet over low heat. Place salmon fillets, skin side down, in skillet; season with salt and pepper. Cover skillet tightly and simmer until salmon is opaque in center, about 8 minutes per inch of thickness. Remove from heat and cool salmon in liquid 5 minutes. Transfer salmon to platter. Cover with plastic wrap and refrigerate at least 4 hours. Serve with reserved watercress mayonnaise.

# PHYLLO-WRAPPED SALMON

*This recipe can be prepared up to 6 hours ahead. Refrigerate and bake as needed.*

½ cup (1 stick) butter
4 cups thinly sliced red bell peppers
1 large leek, white part only, washed and
    thinly sliced
½ cup dry white wine
1 tsp. hot red pepper flakes

½ cup chopped fresh basil
1 tsp. salt
12 sheets phyllo dough
6 salmon fillets (5 oz. each), boned and
    skinned

Melt 2 tbs. of the butter in a skillet over medium heat. Add bell peppers and leek and sauté until tender, about 5 minutes. Add wine and hot red pepper flakes to skillet. Simmer until liquid evaporates. Transfer pepper-leek mixture to a bowl. Stir in basil and salt.

Heat oven to 400°. Melt remaining 6 tbs. butter in a saucepan. Place 1 phyllo sheet on a work surface. Brush with melted butter. Top with a second phyllo sheet; brush with butter. Place 1 fillet crosswise on phyllo sheets. Top salmon with a heaping tbs. of pepper-leek mixture. Fold in sides of phyllo and roll salmon to enclose in pastry, forming a packet. Transfer to a baking sheet, vegetable side up. Brush packet with butter. Repeat with remaining phyllo sheets, salmon and vegetables. Bake until pastry is pale golden, about 30 minutes.

# SALMON BONNE FEMME

*Use either salmon steaks or fillets for this recipe. Garnish with fresh parsley.*

4 salmon steaks (8 oz. each), or 6 fillets (6
  oz. each), boned and skinned
$\frac{1}{2}$ tsp. salt
$\frac{1}{4}$ tsp. pepper
3 tbs. butter, softened, divided

2 tsp. olive oil
2 tbs. chopped shallots or onion
$\frac{3}{4}$ cup dry white wine
$\frac{1}{2}$ cup heavy cream
2 tbs. flour

Season salmon with salt and pepper. Heat 1 tbs. of the butter and oil in a skillet over medium heat. Brown salmon for about 5 minutes on each side until salmon is cooked through. Transfer salmon to a platter. Remove and discard bones and skin if using salmon steaks. Keep warm.

Sprinkle shallots in the skillet over low heat and cook for 2 to 3 minutes. Add wine, increase heat to medium-high and cook to reduce wine by half. Pour in cream and boil for 5 minutes. In a small bowl, blend remaining 2 tbs. butter and flour to form a smooth paste. Whisk butter-flour mixture a small amount at a time into the boiling liquid until sauce is smooth and medium thick. Season with salt and pepper. Reduce heat to low and simmer for 5 minutes. Pour sauce through a strainer. Drizzle sauce over hot salmon.

# SALMON EN CROÛTE

*This impressive dish is actually quick and simple to make. Find puff pastry in the freezer section of your grocery store. If you're making this dish ahead of time, cut steam vents in the pastry before baking to prevent it from becoming soggy.*

1/2 pkg. (1 sheet) puff pastry, thawed
1 pkg. (5 oz.) fresh baby spinach
2 salmon fillets (1-inch thick, 1 1/2-inches wide), boned and skinned
1/4 tsp. salt
2 tbs. purchased mushroom or olive tapenade or pesto, or use *Pesto Sauce,* page 151
1 egg, beaten

Heat oven to 375°. Line a baking sheet with parchment paper or aluminum foil and set aside. Roll out puff pastry on a lightly floured surface to 1/8-inch thick. Place half the spinach lengthwise down center of pastry. Season salmon with salt and place in 1 layer on top of spinach. Spread tapenade over fish and top with remaining spinach. Wrap salmon and spinach in the pastry, folding in edges to seal completely. Place on prepared baking sheet and brush with egg. Bake until pastry is golden brown, about 25 to 30 minutes. Serve immediately.

# SALMON IN RED WINE SAUCE

*The vibrant red wine sauce goes very well with salmon.*

1¼ cups dry red wine
5 tbs. red wine vinegar
2 shallots, minced, or ¼ cup minced onion
4 fresh thyme sprigs
1 tbs. butter

1 tbs. olive oil
6 salmon fillets (8 oz. each)
¾ cup (1½ sticks) cold butter, cut into
   pieces

In a small non-aluminum saucepan over medium-high heat, boil wine, vinegar, shallots and thyme until liquid is reduced to ⅓ cup. Discard thyme. Keep sauce warm.

Heat oven to 200°. Melt 1 tbs. butter with oil in a skillet over medium heat. Add 3 of the salmon fillets and cook until browned and cooked through. Transfer to a baking sheet and place in oven. Repeat with remaining salmon.

Bring sauce to a simmer over low heat. Remove from heat and whisk in 2 tbs. of the cold butter. Set back on heat and whisk in remaining butter 1 tbs. at a time. Pour sauce through a strainer and serve with salmon.

# SALMON TERIYAKI

Makes 4 servings

*Serve this Asian-flavored salmon with steamed rice and snow peas.*

4 salmon fillets (5 oz. each)
salt and pepper to taste
1/2 cup cornstarch
3 tbs. vegetable oil, divided
2 cloves garlic, minced

2 strips orange zest, minced
1/2 tsp. hot red pepper flakes
1 tbs. sesame seeds
2 tbs. soy sauce
2 tbs. water

Sprinkle salmon fillets with salt and pepper. Spread cornstarch in a shallow dish. Dip fillets in cornstarch, coating them all over. Dust off excess cornstarch.

Heat 2 tbs. of the oil in a large skillet over medium heat. Add fish (do not crowd fillets) and cook, in batches if necessary, for about 5 minutes, or until each side is browned and fish is cooked through. Transfer salmon to a platter and keep warm.

Add remaining 1 tbs. oil to the skillet over medium heat; add garlic, orange zest, red pepper flakes and sesame seeds. Cook 1 minute, stirring. Add soy sauce and water. Cook for 30 seconds. Drizzle sauce over each fish fillet.

# SALMON WITH RIESLING-CAPER SAUCE

*This recipe goes equally well with a dry German Riesling wine or a red wine.*

4 salmon fillets (5 oz. each), boned and skinned
2 tbs. low-sodium soy sauce
2 tbs. olive oil, divided
1 large clove garlic, sliced
1 medium red bell pepper, diced

1 medium yellow bell pepper, diced
$\frac{1}{2}$ cup dry Riesling or dry red wine
$\frac{1}{2}$ cup heavy cream
1 tbs. Dijon mustard
2 tbs. capers with brine

Rub salmon with soy sauce and refrigerate for 30 minutes. In a large heavy skillet, heat 1 tbs. of the oil and cook garlic over medium heat until garlic turns light brown, about 2 minutes. Discard garlic. Add bell peppers to skillet and cook for 5 minutes. Add wine and bring to a boil; cook to reduce wine by half. Add cream and return to a boil. Reduce heat to low and simmer for 6 to 8 minutes to thicken sauce. Stir in mustard and capers. Keep sauce warm.

Heat oven to 450°. Add remaining 1 tbs. oil to a large nonstick skillet over high heat. Sear salmon on 1 side, about 2 minutes, and transfer to a baking pan, seared side down. Bake salmon for 5 to 8 minutes, until salmon is just cooked through. Serve sauce over salmon.

# SEARED SALMON WITH THAI VEGETABLES

Makes 4 servings

*The spice rub is also delicious on chicken or other types of fish.*

1 tsp. each chili powder, curry powder, ground coriander, ground cumin, dry mustard, salt
2 tsp. sugar, divided
4 salmon fillets (6 oz. each), with skin
6 tbs. rice vinegar
3 tbs. soy sauce
1 tbs. sesame oil

2 tbs. chopped fresh cilantro
1 tbs. finely chopped fresh ginger
1 tbs. butter
1 cup basmati rice
1 1/3 cups water
2/3 cup canned unsweetened coconut milk
2 tbs. vegetable oil
*Thai Vegetables*, page 83

Mix chili powder, curry, coriander, cumin, mustard, salt and 1 tsp. of the sugar in a small bowl. Sprinkle 1 1/2 tsp. of the spice mixture over flesh side of each fillet. Cover and refrigerate at least 3 hours or overnight. Whisk vinegar, soy sauce, sesame oil, cilantro, ginger and remaining 1 tsp. sugar in a bowl; set aside.

Melt butter in a saucepan over medium heat. Add rice and sauté for 2 minutes. Stir in water and coconut milk and bring to a boil. Cover and reduce heat to low; cook until rice is tender and liquid is absorbed, about 18 minutes. Season with salt and pepper.

While rice cooks, heat vegetable oil in large skillet over medium-high heat. Add salmon fillets, flesh side down. Sear until browned and salmon is just cooked through, about 3 minutes on each side.

Spoon rice onto plates. Top each serving with a seared fillet, then *Thai Vegetables*. Drizzle reserved dressing around and serve immediately, passing extra dressing separately.

## THAI VEGETABLES

1 tbs. sesame oil
2 tsp. minced fresh ginger
1 large clove garlic, minced
1 red bell pepper, thinly sliced
6 oz. shiitake mushrooms, stemmed, thinly sliced

3 large scallions, thinly sliced
3 cups thinly sliced bok choy (leafy tops only)
salt and pepper to taste

Heat oil in a skillet over high heat. Add ginger and garlic; sauté for 20 seconds. Add bell pepper and mushrooms; sauté until pepper is crisp-tender, about 3 minutes. Add scallions and bok choy and sauté until just wilted, about 2 minutes. Season with salt and pepper.

# SALMON FILLETS WITH
# MUSTARD-HORSERADISH VINAIGRETTE

*This entrée is remarkable for its simplicity and full flavor.*

6 salmon fillets (6 oz. each), boned and
    skinned
salt and pepper to taste
¼ cup olive oil, divided

3 tbs. white wine vinegar
2 tbs. Dijon mustard
3 tbs. horseradish, drained

Season salmon with salt and pepper. In a heavy skillet, heat 2 tbs. of the oil over medium-high heat until hot but not smoking. Sear salmon for 5 minutes. Flip salmon and cook for 3 to 4 minutes longer, or until just cooked through.

While salmon is cooking, in a small bowl whisk vinegar, mustard and horseradish with the remaining 2 tbs. oil, salt and pepper until emulsified. Spoon vinaigrette over hot salmon and serve at once.

# STUFFED SALMON FILLET

*This recipe is also delicious served cold with* Sauce Verte, *page 146.*

1 salmon fillet (2 lb.), skinned and boned
salt and pepper to taste
1 cup fresh breadcrumbs
1 cup slivered almonds
1 cup chopped fresh parsley
1 tsp. dried tarragon

3 tbs. grated lemon zest
$1/4$ cup plus 2 tbs. lemon juice, divided
$1/2$ cup (1 stick) butter, softened
cayenne pepper to taste
2 tbs. butter, melted
1 cup dry white wine

Heat oven to 350°. Cut fillet in 2 equal pieces. Season with salt and pepper; set aside. Combine breadcrumbs, almonds and parsley in a food processor workbowl. Process until coarsely chopped. Blend in tarragon, lemon zest, $1/4$ cup of the lemon juice and softened butter. Season with salt, pepper and cayenne. Spoon breadcrumb mixture over the surface of 1 fillet. Top with second fillet, pressing fillet to adhere to stuffing. Tie stuffed fillets with butcher twine. Place fish in a baking pan. Measure stuffed salmon at the thickest part. Pour remaining 2 tbs. lemon juice, melted butter and wine over surface of fish. Bake about 15 minutes per inch of thickness, until flesh is barely opaque throughout. Reserve cooking liquid. Cut fish crosswise into 1- to $1^1/2$-inch-thick slices. Spoon cooking liquid over each portion. Serve hot.

# SALMON STEAKS
# WITH APRICOT-HORSERADISH SAUCE

*This is a really simple recipe with a sweet-and-sour combination of apricot jam, horseradish and vinegar.*

1/4 cup apricot jam
2 tsp. grated horseradish
1 tsp. white vinegar
4 salmon steaks (8 oz. each)
4 sprigs fresh parsley, for garnish

Heat oven to 400°. In a small bowl, combine apricot jam, horseradish and vinegar. Lay salmon in 1 layer in a lightly oiled baking pan. Spoon apricot sauce evenly over tops of salmon. Bake salmon steaks for 10 minutes, until fish flakes when tested with a fork. Skin and bone salmon steaks before serving. Garnish with parsley.

# SALMON WITH GINGER RATATOUILLE

*Influenced by Provençale cuisine, the salmon is immersed in a flavorful vegetable stew.*

1 tbs. olive oil
1 small onion, thinly sliced
2 cloves garlic, minced
2 tbs. finely chopped fresh ginger
1/2 cup diced eggplant
1/2 cup diced zucchini

1/2 cup diced red bell pepper
1 large tomato, seeded and diced
salt and pepper to taste
4 salmon steaks, about 1-inch thick
2 tsp. lemon juice
2 tbs. chopped fresh parsley, for garnish

Heat oven to 350°. In a large skillet heat oil over medium-high heat. Add onion, garlic and ginger and cook, stirring, until onion is soft. Add eggplant, zucchini, bell pepper and tomato. Reduce heat to low and cook gently for 7 to 8 minutes until vegetables are just tender. Season with salt and pepper. Set aside.

Butter a shallow baking pan and place salmon steaks so they are not touching. Pour lemon juice over salmon. Spoon vegetables over and around salmon steaks and cover dish tightly with foil. Bake for 20 minutes, or until salmon flakes easily when tested with a fork. Garnish with parsley.

# BRAISED SALMON STEAKS WITH FENNEL

Makes 4 servings

*The sliced fennel releases a mild anise aroma which complements the braised salmon.*

1 lb. fennel bulbs
1 tbs. olive oil
2 tbs. chopped fresh thyme, or 2 tsp. dried, divided
1/4 cup white wine
salt and pepper to taste
4 salmon steaks (8 oz. each)

Heat oven to 400°. Trim and discard root end and stalks of the fennel bulbs. Cut bulbs across into thin slices. Heat oil in a skillet over medium heat. Add fennel and sauté about 5 minutes, until softened. Add 1 tbs. of the thyme, wine, salt and pepper and cook for 2 minutes.

Transfer fennel to a buttered baking pan. Arrange salmon steaks on top and season with salt, pepper and the remaining thyme. Cover dish with foil and bake for 10 to 12 minutes, until salmon is just cooked through.

Transfer salmon steaks to plates. Cover with fennel and pan juices. Serve hot.

# BROILED PACIFIC SALMON STEAKS
# WITH SALSA BUTTER

*The salmon steaks are marinated in salsa, lime juice, mustard and garlic, imparting a piquant flavor to the fish. Salmon fillets are also suitable for this recipe.*

½ cup  purchased spicy tomato salsa
¼ cup lime juice
1 tsp. Dijon mustard
1 clove garlic, minced
4 salmon steaks (6 oz. each)

¼ cup (½ stick) butter, softened
¾ tsp. grated lime zest
¼ tsp. ground cumin
salt and pepper to taste
lime wedges, for garnish

Set aside 2 tbs. of salsa. In a medium bowl, combine remaining salsa, lime juice, mustard and garlic. Coat salmon steaks with marinade. Cover and refrigerate for at least ½ hour.

Heat broiler on high. In a small bowl, combine butter with lime zest, cumin and the remaining 2 tbs.salsa. Mix well and set aside. Remove salmon steaks from marinade (discard marinade). Season salmon with salt and pepper. Arrange in an oiled pan and place under the broiler, 4 inches from the heat source. Broil 3 minutes per side, or until fish just flakes when tested with a fork. Serve with reserved salsa butter and lime wedges.

# COLD POACHED SALMON STEAKS

*Prepare this recipe a day in advance, and enjoy it with any of the cold sauces in the* Marinades and Sauces *section, page 122.*

3 qt. *Court Bouillon,* page 125
6 salmon steaks (8 oz. each)
1 cup grated cucumber
1 cup sour cream
1 tsp. minced scallion

1½ tsp. lemon juice
¾ tsp. salt
¼ tsp. pepper
½ tsp. chopped fresh dill, for garnish

Bring *Court Bouillon* to a boil over high heat in a large stockpot or skillet with a lid. Add salmon steaks, in 1 layer if possible. Reduce heat to low, cover, and poach for 6 minutes per inch of thickness.

Remove from heat, uncover, and cool fish in poaching liquid for 30 minutes. Remove salmon, discarding liquid. Remove and discard skin and bones; refrigerate salmon.

Arrange salmon on plates or a platter. Combine cucumber, sour cream, scallion, lemon juice, salt and pepper in a small bowl. Spoon over salmon. Sprinkle with chopped dill.

# SALMON STEAKS IN WHITE WINE SAUCE

*The classic white wine sauce is tailor-made for poached or baked salmon.*

6 salmon steaks (8 oz. each)
salt and pepper to taste
2 tsp. olive oil
2 tbs. plus 1 tsp. butter, softened, divided

2 tbs. chopped shallots or onion
1½ cups dry white wine
¾ cup heavy cream
2 tsp. flour

Season salmon with salt and pepper. Heat oil and 2 tsp. of the butter in a skillet over medium heat. Add salmon and brown for 2 minutes on each side. Add shallots and wine and simmer for 10 minutes. Transfer salmon to a platter; cover with foil and keep warm.

Strain cooking liquid into a saucepan over medium-high heat. Add cream and boil for 5 minutes. Mash remaining 1½ tbs. butter with flour in a small bowl to form a smooth paste. Whisk butter mixture a bit at a time into the boiling sauce. Cook until sauce is smooth and medium thick. Season with salt and pepper. Reduce heat to low and simmer sauce for about 10 minutes.

Bone and skin salmon steaks. Pour sauce over salmon and serve at once.

# POACHED SALMON STEAKS
# WITH MUSTARD-PARSLEY SAUCE

Makes 6 servings

*Garnish each plate with small boiled potatoes and sautéed vegetables. Serve hot.*

1 cup dry white wine
1 cup water
1/2 tsp. peppercorns
1 sprig fresh dill
1/2 tsp. salt
6 salmon steaks (8 oz. each)
salt and pepper to taste

2 tbs. butter
2 tbs. flour
2 cups half-and-half
1 tbs. Dijon mustard
1 egg yolk
1/3 cup chopped fresh parsley

Place wine, water, peppercorns, dill and salt in a saucepan or skillet large enough to hold salmon in 1 layer. Bring to a boil over high heat, then reduce heat to low and simmer for 10 minutes.

Measure the thickness of salmon steaks. Season with salt and pepper. Arrange salmon steaks in the pan and poach over low heat for 8 minutes per inch of thickness.

Remove salmon; strain cooking liquid and set aside. Remove and discard bones and skin from salmon; transfer salmon to a platter. Keep warm.

Melt butter in a saucepan over medium heat. Stir in flour and cook, stirring occasionally, for 2 to 3 minutes. Gradually stir in reserved cooking liquid and half-and-half. Cook, whisking, until sauce is thick. Whisk in mustard. Season with salt and pepper and remove from heat.

Place egg yolk in a bowl and beat lightly. Whisk a little of the hot sauce into egg yolk. Pour yolk mixture back into hot sauce. Place back over medium heat and cook, stirring, for 1 minute. Strain sauce. Add parsley. Serve sauce over hot salmon steaks.

# SALMON STEAKS EN PAPILLOTE

Makes 6 servings

*Serve these salmon steaks with* Hollandaise Sauce, *page 130.*

6 salmon steaks (7 oz. each)
salt and pepper to taste
1 tbs. lemon juice
6 slices bacon
18 juniper berries, optional
1 tbs. butter, melted

Heat oven to 400°. Season salmon steaks with salt, pepper and lemon juice. Wrap a slice of bacon around each steak. Place 3 juniper berries, if using, on top of each steak.

Cut 6 sheets of parchment paper to about 12 x 20 inches; fold each sheet in half (to 10 x 12 inches), then open back up. Place each steak in center of 1 side of a sheet of parchment paper. Fold other side of parchment paper over. Fold and crease edges to seal packet well. Brush paper with melted butter to prevent burning.

Arrange salmon packages on a baking sheet and bake for 15 to 20 minutes. The packets will be puffed and brown. Open packets, remove and discard bacon, and serve immediately.

# SALMON STEAKS ITALIENNE

*This dish makes good use of a robust tomato-based sauce.*

1½ tbs. chopped shallots or onion
6 oz. white mushrooms, sliced
6 salmon steaks (8 oz. each)
1½ cups dry white wine
¾ cup *Fish Stock*, page 126

1 can (12 oz.) stewed tomatoes
½ cup diced green bell pepper
2 tsp. flour
2 tsp. butter, softened

Heat oven to 350°. Butter a baking pan large enough to hold salmon steaks in 1 layer. Sprinkle shallots and mushrooms on bottom of pan. Arrange salmon over shallots and mushrooms. Pour wine and *Fish Stock* over and add stewed tomatoes and bell pepper. Bring to a boil on the stove over medium heat. Cover pan with foil, transfer to oven and bake for 10 to 12 minutes.

Skin and bone steaks. Transfer to a serving platter and keep warm. Pour cooking liquid through a strainer into a saucepan over medium-high heat and boil for 10 minutes. In a small bowl, mash together flour and butter to make a smooth paste and whisk into the sauce a bit at a time. Cook sauce, whisking, until it is smooth and medium thick. Cover salmon with sauce and serve at once.

# SALMON STEAKS IN CHAMPAGNE SAUCE

*This dish is the ultimate in elegance, yet is simple to prepare.*

6 salmon steaks (8 oz. each)
1 tbs. minced shallot or onion
2 cups *Fish Stock*, page 126
1 bottle dry champagne (3 cups)

2 tbs. butter, softened
2 tbs. flour
1 egg yolk
1/2 cup heavy cream

Heat oven to 350°. Lay steaks in a baking pan. Sprinkle shallots over steaks, cover with *Fish Stock* and champagne. Bring the liquid to a boil on the stove over medium-high heat. Transfer pan to oven and bake for 10 minutes, until salmon is cooked through. Remove and discard skin and bones from salmon. Transfer salmon to a platter, cover with foil and keep warm. Reserve 1 cup of the cooking liquid.

Melt butter in a saucepan over medium heat, and stir in flour. Whisk in reserved cooking liquid and simmer sauce until slightly thickened. In a bowl, whisk together egg yolk and cream. Whisk 1/2 cup of the hot sauce into cream mixture, then pour cream mixture into hot sauce in saucepan. Reduce heat to low and simmer, whisking, for 2 minutes. Serve sauce with salmon.

# SALMON TORTILLAS

*These are a healthier and more delicious version of fish tacos.*

1 1/2 tsp. chili powder
2 tbs. tequila
1 tbs. lime juice
1/4 tsp. salt
1 1/2 lb. salmon steaks, 3/4- to 1-inch thick
1/3 cup heavy cream

3 tbs. sour cream
2 cups *Salsa Verde*, page 150
12 corn or flour tortillas (8-inch)
1 cucumber, cut into matchsticks
1 1/2 cups chopped fresh cilantro

Heat oven to 375°. In a glass or ceramic baking pan large enough to hold salmon in 1 layer, combine chili powder, tequila, lime juice and salt. Place salmon in pan and turn to coat. Marinate for 10 minutes. Bake for 12 to 14 minutes, until cooked through. Set aside and keep warm. Reduce oven to 300°. In a bowl whisk cream and sour cream. Set aside.

Place *Salsa Verde* in a shallow bowl. Dip tortillas in salsa to coat both sides, shake off excess, and lay them on a foiled-lined baking sheet. Heat in oven until warmed through. Break salmon into bite-sized pieces, discarding skin and bones. Place salmon in center of each tortilla. Top with cucumber, cilantro, remaining *Salsa Verde* and reserved cream mixture. Fold and serve immediately.

# SALMON ROAST WITH LENTILS

Makes 6 servings

*For the bouquet garni, tie together 2 sprigs of parsley, a sprig of thyme and a bay leaf with a piece of string. Or if you don't have fresh herbs, combine a few tablespoons each of dried parsley and thyme with the bay leaf and wrap in a square of cheesecloth.*

8 oz. dry lentils
3 whole cloves
1 medium onion, peeled
1 whole clove garlic
1 bouquet garni
2 cups water
salt and pepper to taste

1 piece center-cut salmon with bone (4 lb.)
1/4 lb. bacon, sliced
1 1/2 cups heavy cream
2 tbs. grated horseradish
2 shallots, chopped, or 1/4 cup chopped onion

Rinse lentils well in cold water. Push cloves into onion and place in a saucepan with lentils. Add garlic and bouquet garni. Cover with water. Bring to a boil over high heat. Cover, reduce heat to low and simmer for 30 minutes, stirring occasionally. Add more water if lentils seem dry and continue simmering until tender, 20 to 30 minutes longer. Most of the water should be absorbed. If necessary, remove the lid toward the end of cooking to allow water to evaporate. Discard onion, bouquet garni and garlic. Season lentils to taste with salt and pepper. Keep hot.

Heat oven to 425°. Scale salmon if necessary and rinse under cold water. Measure fish at its thickest point. Place in a baking pan. Season with salt and pepper. Wrap salmon with bacon. Roast in oven for 10 minutes per inch of thickness, basting occasionally with the drippings in the pan.

Transfer salmon to a serving platter. Remove bacon and skin of the fish. Cover loosely with foil and keep warm. Discard fat from the baking pan, add cream to the pan and bring to a boil over medium heat, stirring with a spoon to dissolve pan juices. Pour sauce through a strainer into a saucepan. Add horseradish and shallots. Bring back to a boil over medium-high heat, reduce heat to low and simmer for 5 minutes.

Spoon lentils around salmon. Serve sauce separately.

# BAKED WHOLE SALMON

*Attention salmon angler: If your catch of the day is a 3- to 6-pound salmon, you've found the right recipe. Garnish the salmon with sautéed mushroom caps.*

1 whole salmon (5 lb.), cleaned and scaled
salt and pepper to taste
3 tbs. chopped shallots or onion
2 cups *Fish Stock*, page 126

2 cups white wine
2 tbs. butter, softened
1/4 cup flour

Heat oven to 425°. Place salmon flat in a baking pan large enough to hold it. Season cavity with salt and pepper. Sprinkle shallots around fish. Pour *Fish Stock* and wine in pan. Measure salmon at its thickest part. Bake for 12 minutes per inch of thickness, basting occasionally with liquid in pan.

Transfer salmon to a large serving platter. Remove skin from top side. Cover salmon with foil and keep warm. Strain cooking liquid into a saucepan over medium-high heat and boil until reduced to 2 cups. Combine butter and flour in a small bowl to form a smooth paste and whisk into boiling liquid a bit at a time to make a creamy sauce. Season to taste. Pour any juice from the platter into sauce. Reduce sauce to a medium-thick consistency. Pour a small amount over salmon.

Starting at the tail end, use a knife and fork to cut top fillet into serving portions. Slide knife between fillet and bone to lift the portions. Before serving bottom fillet, lift off tail and pull backbone away from flesh, removing backbone and head all in 1 piece. Bottom fillet is now boneless and easy to lift into serving-size portions. Free skin from portions before serving. Spoon sauce over salmon.

*Sockeye Salmon*

# BRAISED BLUEBACK SALMON
# WITH WHITE WINE SAUCE

*The blueback salmon is the Pacific sockeye salmon. A bouquet garni is a bunch of herbs tied together or placed in cheesecloth so that it can be removed easily after cooking.*

¼ cup (½ stick) butter, divided
5 medium shallots, minced, or ½ cup
 minced onion
1 whole salmon (5 lb.), cleaned and scaled
3 cups dry white wine

salt and pepper to taste
1 bouquet garni (parsley, basil, bay leaves)
4 egg yolks
1 cup heavy cream

Heat oven to 425°. Melt 2 tbs. of the butter in a saucepan over medium heat. Add shallots and cook until golden. Spread shallots into a baking pan large enough to hold salmon. Place salmon flat in the baking pan. Season cavity with salt and pepper. Add bouquet garni to the cavity. Dot fish with remaining 2 tbs. butter.

Measure salmon at its thickest part. Cover pan with foil and bake for 12 minutes per inch of thickness. Baste fish occasionally with liquid in the baking pan.

Transfer salmon to a large platter. Remove skin from top side. Cover with foil and keep warm. Strain cooking liquid into a small saucepan over medium-high heat and boil to reduce to 2 cups. Beat egg yolks with cream in a small bowl. Reduce heat to low and whisk cream mixture slowly into sauce. Cook, whisking often, until sauce thickens slightly. Do not boil the sauce as it may separate. Season with salt and pepper. Keep warm.

Starting at the tail end of the salmon, use a knife and fork to cut top fillet into serving portions. Slide knife between fillet and bone to lift the portions. Before serving bottom fillet, lift off tail and pull backbone away from flesh, removing backbone and head all in 1 piece. Bottom fillet is now boneless and easy to lift into serving size portions. Free skin from portions before serving. Spoon sauce over salmon.

# GRILLED WHOLE SALMON
# WITH LEMON-RICE STUFFING

Makes 6 servings

*A wire grill basket is helpful when grilling whole salmon. The special basket makes a small whole salmon easy to turn over.*

½ cup (1 stick) butter, divided
½ cup chopped onion
½ cup chopped celery
3 cups cooked white rice
1 tsp. grated lemon zest

¼ cup plus 1 tbs. lemon juice, divided
⅓ cup slivered almonds, toasted
1 whole salmon (5 lb.), cleaned and scaled
salt and pepper to taste
lemon wedges, for garnish

In a large saucepan, melt ¼ cup of the butter over medium heat; add onion and celery and sauté until tender. Stir in rice, lemon zest, 2 tbs. of the lemon juice and almonds. Mix well. Set aside.

Prepare a medium fire on a grill. Brush cavity of the salmon with 1 tbs. of the lemon juice and season lightly with salt and pepper. Stuff salmon loosely with about 1 cup of the reserved lemon-rice stuffing. Skewer cavity closed.

In a small saucepan, melt remaining ¼ cup butter and stir in remaining 2 tbs. lemon juice. Brush over outside of fish. Place in a greased wire fish basket on the grill. Cover grill and cook salmon for about 20 minutes. Turn salmon and continue cooking for about 15 to 20 minutes, or until salmon flakes easily when tested with a fork. Baste salmon occasionally with remaining lemon-butter mixture. Meanwhile, heat remaining lemon-rice stuffing.

Remove skewers from salmon. Serve with remaining lemon rice. Garnish with lemon wedges.

Pink Salmon

# TOURNEDOS OF SALMON

*These salmon rolls can be prepared up to a day ahead. Refrigerate, then bake in the oven just before serving. Serve with* Dill Piccata Sauce, *page 133.*

6 salmon steaks (6–7 oz. each), cut ³/₄-inch thick, boned and skinned
2 tbs. chopped scallions (white and green parts)

2 tbs. chopped fresh dill
3 flour tortillas (about 10-inch)
salt and pepper to taste
fresh dill and lemon wedges, for garnish

Heat oven to 400°. Place each salmon steak on a work surface skin side down in a long strip. (Some of the steaks will break into 2 pieces when boned; line the pieces up in 1 long strip.) Sprinkle each with 1 tsp. of the scallions and 1 tsp. of the dill. Roll up jelly-roll fashion. Place flat side down. Cut each tortilla into 4 strips 1-inch wide (discard the ends). Wrap 2 tortilla strips around each salmon roll. Secure ends with toothpicks. Transfer salmon rolls to greased baking sheets, placing them at least 1¹/₂ inches apart. Sprinkle salmon rolls with salt and pepper. Bake for 15 minutes, or until cooked through. Garnish with sprigs of fresh dill and lemon wedges.

# STEELHEAD NAPA VALLEY

*Steelhead trout are in the salmon family. Substitute a whole salmon if you wish, and use any favorite dry white wine. Serve this dish with steamed asparagus.*

1 whole steelhead (4 lb.), cleaned and
  scaled
1½ cups *Fish Fumet*, page 126
1½ cups Napa Valley dry white wine
1 cup heavy cream
2 tbs. butter, softened, divided

1 tbs. flour
salt and pepper to taste
8 oz. white mushrooms, stemmed
8 oz. pearl onions, peeled
1 tbs. chopped fresh parsley, for garnish
1 tbs. chopped fresh sage, for garnish

Measure fish at its thickest point and place in a large skillet. Pour Fish Fumet and wine over fish. Cover, place over medium-low heat and simmer 10 minutes per inch of thickness. Remove fish to a platter; keep warm. Strain cooking liquid into a saucepan over medium heat and cook until reduced by half. Add cream and cook for 5 minutes. In a small bowl, mix 1 tbs. of the butter with flour into a smooth paste. Whisk into sauce a bit at a time until sauce is thickened. Reduce heat to low and simmer for 10 minutes. Season with salt and pepper.

In a skillet over medium heat, sauté mushrooms in remaining 1 tbs. butter for 5 minutes. Cook pearl onions in salted boiling water until tender. Drain and add to sauce along with mushrooms. Pour mushroom sauce over steelhead. Sprinkle herbs over fish and serve hot.

# WHOLE ROASTED SALMON
# WITH WILD RICE STUFFING

*A 4-pound center-cut piece of salmon can also be used for this recipe.*

2¹/₂ cups cold water
1 cup wild rice, rinsed
1 tsp. salt, divided
2 tbs. butter
1 cup chopped white mushrooms
¹/₂ cup chopped onion
1 clove garlic, minced
¹/₂ cup slivered almonds

1 tsp. dried thyme
¹/₂ tsp. dried sage
¹/₄ tsp. pepper
2 tbs. lemon juice, divided
1 whole salmon (5 lb.), cleaned and scaled
1 tbs. butter, melted
8 lemon wedges, for garnish

Heat oven to 425°. In a saucepan over high heat, combine water, wild rice and ¹/₂ tsp. of the salt. Cover and bring to a boil. Reduce heat to low, cover, and simmer for 40 to 50 minutes, or until rice is tender and no liquid remains. Transfer to a bowl and set aside to cool.

Melt 2 tbs. butter in a skillet; add mushrooms, onion, garlic, almonds, thyme, sage and pepper. Cook until onions are tender. Add to rice along with 1 tbs. of the lemon juice.

Brush cavity of salmon with remaining 1 tbs. lemon juice. Sprinkle with remaining ½ tsp. salt. Place on a rimmed baking sheet. Fill cavity loosely with about 1 cup of the wild rice mixture. Place remaining wild rice mixture in a baking dish and cover.

Arrange the stuffed salmon in a "swimming position" (on its stomach). Place crumpled foil around fish, if necessary, to hold it in place. Brush fish with melted butter. Measure salmon at its thickest part. Bake for 12 minutes per inch of thickness. Place wild rice mixture in oven along with fish to heat through.

Transfer salmon to a platter. Carefully remove skin from both sides of salmon. Garnish with lemon wedges. Arrange hot wild rice around salmon.

Rainbow Trout

# WHOLE SALMON WITH CREAM SAUCE

*A 4-pound center-cut piece of salmon can also be used for this recipe. Garnish with sautéed mushroom caps.*

1 whole salmon (5 lb.), cleaned and scaled
salt and pepper to taste
3 tbs. chopped shallots or onion
2 cups *Fish Stock*, page 126
2 cups white wine
2 tbs. butter, softened
1/4 cup flour

Heat oven to 425°. Place salmon lying flat in a baking pan large enough to hold it. Season cavity with salt and pepper. Sprinkle shallots around salmon.

Pour *Fish Stock* and wine in the pan. Measure salmon at its thickest part. Bake for 12 minutes per inch of thickness. Baste fish occasionally with liquid in pan.

Transfer salmon to a large platter. Remove and discard skin from the top side. Cover fish with foil and keep warm. Strain cooking liquid into a saucepan over high heat and cook to reduce to 2 cups.

In a small bowl, combine butter and flour to form a smooth paste. Whisk into boiling liquid a bit at a time to make a creamy sauce. Season with salt and pepper. Pour any juice from the platter into the sauce. Pour a small amount of sauce over salmon.

Starting at the tail end, use a fish knife and fork to cut the top fillet into serving size portions. Slide knife between the salmon fillet and bone to lift the portions. Before serving the bottom fillet, lift off tail and pull backbone away from flesh, removing backbone and head all in 1 piece. Bottom fillet is now boneless and easy to serve into portions. Free the skin from portions before serving. Spoon sauce over salmon. Serve hot.

# MATELOTE OF SALMON

*This French-style fish stew can be prepared a day ahead: When the sauce is poured over the salmon, cool and refrigerate. Bake to reheat before serving. Serve with rice or noodles.*

$1/2$ lb. small pearl onions, peeled
1 salmon fillet ($1^1/2$ lb.)
3 tbs. olive oil, divided
salt and pepper to taste
$1/2$ lb. small mushroom caps
1 cup chopped onion
2 tbs. chopped shallots
2 cups dry red wine
3 cups *Fish Stock*, page 126
1 tbs. chopped garlic
$1^1/2$ tbs. butter, softened
$1^1/2$ tbs. flour

Heat oven to 400°. In a saucepan over high heat, place pearl onions and cover with water. Boil onions until just tender, about 4 minutes. Drain and set aside.

Remove and discard skin and bones from salmon and cut across into 12 equal pieces. Heat 2 tbs. of the oil in a skillet over medium heat. Brown salmon pieces on all sides. Season with salt and pepper. Transfer to an ovenproof casserole dish. Cover and keep warm.

Add remaining 1 tbs. oil to skillet with reserved pearl onions and mushroom caps. Sauté until golden brown. Remove from skillet and set aside.

Add chopped onion and shallots to skillet, reduce heat to low and cook for 2 minutes. Pour in wine and *Fish Stock.* Add garlic. Increase heat to medium-high and bring to a boil. Reduce heat to medium-low and simmer until reduced by half. In a small bowl, mash together butter and flour to make a smooth paste; whisk into liquid a bit at a time to thicken the sauce.

Add reserved pearl onions and mushrooms to sauce. Pour sauce over fish in casserole dish and bake for 10 to 12 minutes, or until heated through. Serve hot.

# SALMON AND WILD RICE PIE

*This is a great use for leftover baked or poached salmon. Serve with steamed asparagus and* Beurre Blanc, *page 127.*

³/₄ cup wild rice
5 cups water
2 tbs. butter
4 scallions, sliced
2 cups diced white mushrooms
2 celery stalks, diced
2 tbs. chopped fresh dill

2 tbs. chopped fresh parsley
salt and pepper to taste
1¹/₂ lb. cooked salmon, fresh or canned
4 eggs
1 cup sour cream
pastry for a deep 10-inch double-crust pie

Rinse rice. Place rice in a saucepan with water; bring to a boil over high heat. Reduce heat to low, cover pan and simmer for 45 to 50 minutes, until rice is tender. Drain any remaining liquid and transfer rice to a large bowl.

Heat oven to 400°. Melt butter in a skillet over medium heat. Add scallions, mushrooms and celery. Cook for about 10 minutes, stirring occasionally. Cool slightly. Add to rice with dill, parsley, salt and pepper.

Flake salmon, discarding any skin and bones. Stir into rice mixture.

In a small bowl, beat 3 of the eggs with sour cream. Blend into rice mixture.

On a floured surface, roll out half of the pastry and use it to line a deep-dish 10-inch pie plate. Fill bottom crust with salmon-rice mixture. Roll out remaining pastry. Moisten pastry rim; arrange pastry over filling. Trim and flute edge. Beat remaining egg in a small bowl. Brush over pastry. Cut steam vents in center of pastry. Bake for 15 minutes. Reduce heat to 375°; bake for 35 minutes longer, or until crust is golden brown. Let stand for 30 minutes before serving.

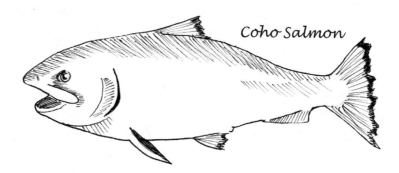

Coho Salmon

# CREAMED SALMON CASSEROLE

*Serve this dish with hot rice or pasta.*

1½ lb. cooked salmon
¼ cup (½ stick) butter
¼ cup chopped onion
8 oz. white mushrooms, sliced
½ cup dry white wine
2 tbs. flour

½ cup milk
½ cup heavy cream
salt and pepper to taste
1 tbs. chopped fresh parsley
½ cup breadcrumbs

Heat oven to 350°. Break up salmon, discarding any skin and bones. Set aside. Melt butter over medium heat in a heavy skillet. Add onion and mushrooms and sauté until tender. Add wine, raise heat to medium-high and cook to reduce liquid by half. Set aside to cool for 5 minutes.

Stir in flour until well combined. Pour in milk and cream. Mix well, place over medium heat and whisk until sauce is thickened and creamy. Season with salt and pepper, reduce heat to low and simmer for 5 minutes. Stir in salmon and heat through. Spoon salmon mixture in a casserole dish. Sprinkle with parsley and breadcrumbs. Bake for 15 minutes. Serve hot.

# SALMON CUTLETS POJARSKY

*Salmon can be transformed into moist and tender chops or cutlets. Serve these with your favorite fish sauce.*

4 slices white bread
1 cup milk
1 salmon fillet (2 lb.)
$\frac{1}{4}$ cup ($\frac{1}{2}$ stick) ) butter, softened
salt and pepper to taste
3 tbs. canola oil

In a bowl, soak bread in milk for 10 minutes. While bread is soaking, skin, bone and cube salmon. Place salmon in a food processor workbowl and coarsely chop. Transfer to a large bowl. Squeeze out excess moisture from bread and mix bread well into salmon. Blend in butter until mixture is smooth. Season with salt and pepper. Shape salmon mixture into 6 thin cutlets.

Heat oil in a nonstick pan over medium heat. Place salmon cutlets into skillet, in batches if necessary. Cook for about 4 to 5 minutes on each side until golden. Serve hot.

# SALMON-IN-A-CRUST

*Feel free to use leftover cooked salmon in this dish, instead of canned. For a touch of whimsy, cut out pastry scraps in the shape of fish to place on top.*

2 cups flour
1 tsp. salt
2 sticks (1 cup) cold butter, divided
5 tbs. cold water
1 cup chopped onions
1 clove garlic, minced
1/2 cup fresh breadcrumbs

1/3 cup grated Parmesan cheese
3 hard-cooked eggs, sliced
1 can (7 1/2 oz.) salmon, drained and flaked
1/3 cup chopped fresh dill
1 cup sour cream
1 egg yolk
1/2 tsp. salt

In a food processor workbowl, combine flour and salt and pulse to blend. Cut 3/4 cup of the butter into small pieces, add to flour and pulse until butter is the size of peas. Add water and pulse to blend just until dough becomes a ball. Wrap dough in plastic wrap and refrigerate for 20 minutes.

Heat oven to 375°. In a skillet over medium heat, sauté onions and garlic in 2 tbs. of the butter until tender. In a small bowl, combine breadcrumbs and cheese.

Divide dough in half, making 1 part slightly larger. Roll out small half on a lightly floured surface to a rectangle ⅛-inch thick and about 7 x 9 inches. Place on a baking sheet. Melt remaining 2 tbs. butter in a small saucepan; set aside.

Leaving a 1-inch border around edge of pastry, sprinkle with ½ of breadcrumb mixture, then ½ of the onion mixture, all the sliced eggs, salmon and dill, then remaining onion mixture and crumb mixture. Drizzle with reserved melted butter and spread with sour cream. Combine egg yolk and salt in a small bowl. Brush pastry borders lightly with egg mixture.

Roll out remaining pastry into a 10 x 12-inch rectangle. Fit over layered filling. Seal and flute edges. Cut shapes with any leftover pieces of pastry to decorate top crust. Brush pastry with remaining egg yolk. Cut slits to allow steam to escape. Bake for about 1 hour or until pastry is golden. Let stand 10 minutes before cutting.

# SALMON FLORENTINE

*This recipe can be prepared in advance, refrigerated and baked half an hour before serving, and may be made in one large dish instead of individual casseroles.*

3 cups cooked flaked salmon
3 cups hot milk
1/3 cup butter
1/3 cup flour
1/2 tsp. dry mustard

1/4 tsp. salt
1/2 tsp. Tabasco Sauce
1 1/2 cups grated Swiss cheese, divided
3 cups spinach, cooked, drained and
   chopped

Heat oven to 425°. Remove any bones or skin from salmon. If canned, drain salmon, save the liquid and add to milk to make 3 cups.

In a saucepan over medium heat, melt butter, add flour and stir with a whisk until well blended. Whisk in milk. Cook, whisking frequently, until sauce is thick and smooth. Season with mustard, salt and Tabasco. Remove from heat and stir in 1 cup of the cheese until melted. Combine salmon with sauce; set aside.

Divide spinach among 6 individual greased casseroles, top with salmon mixture and sprinkle with remaining 1/2 cup cheese. Baked uncovered for 15 minutes, or until cheese is golden brown.

# SALMON PROVENÇALE

*Using ingredients reminiscent of Provence, this healthful dish imparts a wonderful flavor.*

1 tbs. olive oil
1 cup sliced onions
2 cloves garlic, minced
12 black olives, pitted and sliced
2 cups tomato sauce
1½ lb. cooked salmon, boned and skinned
¼ cup breadcrumbs

Heat oven to 350°. Warm oil in a skillet over medium heat. Add onions and sauté until tender. Add garlic, olives and tomato sauce. Simmer for 5 minutes.

Flake salmon into a buttered baking pan. Pour sauce over. Sprinkle with breadcrumbs and bake for 15 minutes until heated through.

# MARINADES AND SAUCES

123 Basic Salmon Marinade
123 Asian Salmon Marinade
124 Spicy Salmon Marinade
125 Court Bouillon
126 Fish Stock
126 Fish Fumet
127 Beurre Blanc
128 Béchamel Sauce
129 Velouté Sauce
130 Hollandaise Sauce
131 Hollandaise Sauce Variations
132 Mornay Sauce
133 Dill Piccata Sauce
134 Cream Sauce with Chives
135 Cucumber Paprika Sauce
136 Red Pepper-Garlic Sauce
137 Red Wine Sauce
138 Sweet and Sour Mayonnaise

138 Dill Mustard Sauce
139 Tarragon Honey-Mustard Dressing
140 Basic Mayonnaise
141 Mayonnaise Variations
142 Creamy Cucumber Dressing
142 Creamy Garlic Sauce
143 Mayonnaise Mustard Sauce
144 Paprika Mayonnaise
145 Remoulade Sauce
146 Sauce Verte
147 Tartar Sauce
148 Tyrolienne Sauce
149 Black Bean and Mango Salsa
150 Salsa Verde
151 Pesto Sauce
151 Mayonnaise Pesto Sauce

# BASIC SALMON MARINADE

Makes about 1½ cups

*This marinade is as delicious on chicken as it is on salmon.*

½ cup dry white wine
1 small onion, finely chopped
½ cup light soy sauce
¼ cup water

1 clove garlic, minced
2 tbs. brown sugar
¼ tsp. pepper
¼ tsp. Tabasco Sauce

Combine all ingredients in a glass container. Store in the refrigerator until ready to use.

# ASIAN SALMON MARINADE

Makes about ¾ cup

*This is an intensely flavored marinade without heat.*

2 cloves garlic, minced
1 tbs. chopped fresh ginger
1 cup fresh cilantro
1 tbs. sugar

½ cup sake or rice wine
1 tbs. sesame oil
1 tsp. salt
¼ tsp. pepper

Puree garlic, ginger and cilantro in a food processor workbowl. Add sugar, sake, sesame oil, salt and pepper and puree until smooth. Refrigerate until ready to use.

# SPICY SALMON MARINADE

*Double or triple this recipe and freeze the extra marinade for future use.*

1 small onion, chopped
1 tbs. brown sugar
1/4 cup cider vinegar
2 tbs. ketchup
2 tbs. dry mustard

1 tsp. Worcestershire sauce
1/4 tsp. ground cloves
1 tsp. chili powder
1/4 tsp. cayenne pepper

Combine onion, brown sugar, vinegar, ketchup, mustard, Worcestershire, cloves, chili powder and cayenne in a saucepan, place over medium heat and boil until reduced to a thin syrup. Pour syrup through a strainer, discard solids and refrigerate the syrup until ready to use.

# COURT BOUILLON

*Keep a supply of court bouillon in your freezer for poaching any fish or chicken.*

2 small leeks
4 medium onions, sliced
3 stalks celery, sliced
2 carrots, sliced
2 cloves garlic, crushed
3½ qt. water
1 cup dry white wine

½ cup white wine vinegar
12 parsley stems
1 tsp. dried thyme
2 bay leaves
1 tsp. cracked black peppercorns
1 tsp. salt

Trim leeks. Split lengthwise, wash thoroughly to remove all grit and slice. Place onions, celery, carrots, leeks, garlic and water in a large stockpot over high heat. Bring to a boil, reduce heat to low and maintain a simmer. Skim off all foam which surfaces. Simmer for 15 minutes.

Add wine, vinegar, parsley stems, thyme, bay leaves, peppercorns and salt. Simmer stock for 15 minutes longer. Pour stock through a strainer; discard solids. Cool to room temperature before refrigerating.

# FISH STOCK

*Your butcher or fishmonger will provide fish bones at very little cost.*

2 lb. lean fish bones or salmon bones
1 small leek
2 medium onions, sliced
2 stalks celery, sliced
1 carrot, sliced
2 cloves garlic, crushed

1 cup dry white wine
2½ qt. water
10 parsley stems
1 tsp. dried thyme
1 bay leaf
1 tsp. cracked black peppercorns

Wash fish bones in cold running water. Discard any fins or tail. Chop bones into large chunks. Trim leek, split lengthwise, wash thoroughly to remove all grit and slice. Put fish bones, onions, celery, carrot, leek, garlic, wine and water in a large stockpot over high heat. Bring to a boil; reduce heat to low to maintain a simmer. Skim off any foam which surfaces.

Add parsley stems, thyme, bay leaf and peppercorns. Simmer stock for 20 to 30 minutes. Pour stock through a strainer; discard solids. Cool stock to room temperature before refrigerating or freezing it. The stock will keep for 3 days in the refrigerator, 2 months in the freezer.

**FISH FUMET:** Place fish stock in a saucepan over high heat and cook until reduced by half.

# BEURRE BLANC (WHITE BUTTER SAUCE)

*This white butter sauce is the perfect accompaniment for poached or grilled salmon.*

3 tbs. white wine vinegar
3 tbs. dry white wine
2 tbs. finely chopped shallots or onion
$\frac{1}{2}$ cup heavy cream
1 cup (2 sticks) butter, cold, cut into pieces
salt and pepper to taste

In a small non-aluminum saucepan over high heat, boil vinegar, wine and shallots until nearly all liquid is evaporated. Add cream, return to a boil and cook until liquid is nearly evaporated and sauce is very thick.

Reduce heat to low and whisk in the cold butter a few pieces at a time. The sauce will become creamy. Do not overheat the sauce, as it will separate and lose its creamy texture. Season with salt and pepper.

Keep the sauce warm over a pan of warm water. Serve as soon as possible.

# BÉCHAMEL SAUCE

Makes about 1 cup

*Béchamel, the base of many other sauces, is often called white or cream sauce. This French sauce is made by stirring milk into a mixture of butter and flour, called a roux. The thickness of the sauce depends on the proportion of flour and butter to milk.*

2 tbs. butter
2 tbs. flour

1¼ cups hot milk
salt and pepper to taste

Melt butter in a heavy saucepan over medium heat. Whisk in flour and cook, stirring constantly, for 1 to 2 minutes; don't let it brown. Whisk in milk, continuing to stir as sauce thickens. Bring sauce to a boil. Add salt and pepper, reduce heat to low and cook, stirring, for 2 to 3 minutes longer. To cool this sauce for later use, cover it with waxed paper to prevent a skin from forming.

NOTE: The amount of flour determines the thickness of the sauce. For a thin sauce: 1 tbs. each of butter and flour per 1 cup milk; medium sauce: 2 tbs. each of butter and flour per 1 cup milk; thick sauce: 3 tbs. each of butter and flour per 1 cup milk.

# VELOUTÉ SAUCE

*A basic sauce on which many other sauces are built, velouté is chicken or fish stock thickened with a flour-and-butter roux.*

1 tbs. butter
2 tbs. flour
2 cups *Fish Stock,* page 126
salt and pepper to taste

Melt butter in a heavy saucepan over medium heat. Whisk in flour and cook, stirring constantly, for 1 to 2 minutes; don't let it brown. Whisk in *Fish Stock,* continuing to stir as sauce thickens. Bring it to a boil. Reduce heat to low and simmer, stirring, for 5 minutes longer. Season with salt and pepper if necessary.

NOTE: Seafood stock mixes, such as Knorr brand and other instant seafood bases, are acceptable substitutes for a homemade fish stock, but do not match the quality.

MARINADES AND SAUCES FOR SALMON   129

# HOLLANDAISE SAUCE

Makes 2$\frac{1}{2}$ cups

*You may clarify the butter before preparing the sauce, if you wish: Melt the butter in a saucepan over medium heat. Skim froth from the surface. Carefully pour off clear, melted butter into another container, discarding the milky solids on the bottom of the pan.*

6 egg yolks
3 tbs. lemon juice
2 tbs. water

1 lb. (4 sticks) butter, melted
$\frac{1}{4}$ tsp. salt
$\frac{1}{2}$ tsp. cayenne pepper

Combine egg yolks, lemon juice, and water in a stainless steel bowl. Using a whisk, beat well. Place a saucepan on low heat; add about 1 inch of water to pan. Bring water to a simmer. Place bowl over pan of water. Beat yolk mixture constantly until it reaches 150° on an instant-read thermometer. Immediately remove the bowl from the hot-water heat source. The mixture should be creamy.

Slowly and gradually beat in melted butter, drop by drop at first to create an emulsion, or smooth sauce. As the emulsion forms, butter can be added more quickly.

When all the butter has been added, adjust seasoning with salt and cayenne pepper. If necessary, thin the sauce by whisking in a few drops of warm water.

Keep the sauce warm over a pot of hot water and serve as soon as possible.

# HOLLANDAISE SAUCE VARIATIONS

**SAUCE MOUSSELINE:** Fold 1/2 cup whipped cream into hollandaise.

**SAUCE MALTAISE:** Add 1/4 cup orange juice and 1/2 tsp grated orange zest to hollandaise.

**SAUCE MOUTARDE:** Add 1 tsp. Dijon mustard to hollandaise.

**HAZELNUT SAUCE:** Mix 1/4 cup ground hazelnuts into hollandaise.

**MACADAMIA SAUCE:** Mix 1/4 cup chopped macadamia nuts into hollandaise.

**MAXIMILIAN SAUCE:** Add 1 tsp. anchovy paste to hollandaise.

# MORNAY SAUCE

*Mornay sauce is a basic béchamel sauce enriched with cheese.*

1 tbs. butter
1 tbs. flour
1 cup hot milk
1 egg yolk
½ cup grated Swiss cheese
½ tsp. salt
¼ tsp. pepper
⅛ tsp. grated nutmeg

Melt butter in a saucepan over medium heat. Whisk in flour and cook for 1 minute. Add milk and cook, whisking often, until sauce is thick. Reduce heat to low, whisk in egg yolk and cook, whisking constantly, for 2 minutes. Add cheese and stir until cheese is melted and sauce is smooth.

Remove sauce from heat. Season with salt, pepper and nutmeg. If not using immediately, pour sauce in a container, cover with waxed paper and refrigerate. Heat before serving.

# DILL PICCATA SAUCE

*This sauce is especially good with* Tournedos of Salmon, *page 106.*

$^1/_2$ cup dry white wine or dry vermouth
$^1/_2$ cup vegetable broth or chicken broth
$1^1/_2$ tbs. lemon juice
$^1/_2$ tbs. heavy cream
1 tbs. cornstarch dissolved in 2 tbs. water
$1^1/_2$ tbs. capers, rinsed
$1^1/_2$ tbs. chopped fresh dill, or $1^1/_2$ tsp. dried
salt and pepper to taste

In a saucepan over medium-low heat, simmer wine, broth, lemon juice and cream for 5 minutes. Remove from heat and whisk in cornstarch mixture. Return to stove, raise heat to medium and bring to a boil, stirring constantly. Stir in capers, dill, salt and pepper.

Sauce may be refrigerated overnight. Reheat before serving.

# CREAM SAUCE WITH CHIVES

*This is a delicious sauce with poached salmon recipes.*

2 tbs. butter
1 tbs. chopped shallot or onion
$\frac{1}{2}$ cup dry white wine
2 tbs. lemon juice
2 tbs. flour

2 cups hot milk
salt and pepper to taste
cayenne pepper to taste
grated nutmeg to taste
$\frac{1}{4}$ cup finely chopped fresh chives

Heat butter in a non-aluminum saucepan over medium-low heat. Add shallots, cover pan and cook for 3 minutes, or until shallots are translucent. Add wine and lemon juice and simmer, uncovered, for 10 minutes, until reduced to a glaze.

Whisk in flour, then milk. Raise heat to medium and bring to a boil while whisking. Reduce heat to low and simmer for 5 minutes. Season with salt, pepper, cayenne and nutmeg. Pour sauce through a strainer, discarding solids. Add chives just before serving.

# CUCUMBER PAPRIKA SAUCE

*Serve this delicate sauce with chicken and salmon.*

2 tbs. olive oil
2 shallots, sliced, or $1/4$ cup sliced onion
$2/3$ cup coarsely chopped cucumber
2 tsp. paprika
1 cup white wine
$1 1/2$ cups heavy cream
salt to taste

Heat olive oil in a medium saucepan over medium heat. Add shallots and cucumber and sauté for 2 to 3 minutes (do not brown). Add paprika and stir to coat well. Add wine and simmer until reduced by about two-thirds. While stirring, slowly add cream. Simmer until sauce is reduced by one-third or it coats the back of the spoon. Season with salt. Pour sauce through a strainer. Serve hot.

# RED PEPPER-GARLIC SAUCE

*Cover salmon fillets or steaks with this sauce, bake, and you have a delicious dish. To roast bell peppers, place them directly on a burner set on high and turn occasionally until skins are black. Place peppers in a bag for 10 minutes to soften peppers and loosen their skins.*

2 medium red bell peppers, roasted
3 tbs. butter, divided
1/2 cup chopped onion
4 cloves garlic, minced
1 cup dry white wine
1 cup *Fish Stock*, page 126

1 chile pepper (jalapeño or Fresno), minced
salt and pepper to taste
1/2 cup diced red bell pepper
1/2 cup peeled, seeded and diced tomatoes
2 tbs. chopped fresh oregano, or 2 tsp. dried
2 tbs. chopped fresh parsley

Discard seeds and skins from roasted peppers. Place peppers in a blender container and puree. Heat 2 tbs. of the butter in a saucepan over medium heat and sauté onion and garlic until lightly browned. Add wine and simmer for 5 minutes. Add bell pepper puree, *Fish Stock* and chile pepper to wine mixture and simmer for 5 minutes. Adjust seasonings and keep warm.

Sauté diced peppers and tomatoes a skillet in remaining 1 tbs. butter over medium heat for 2 minutes. Add pepper-tomato mixture, oregano and parsley to sauce. Serve hot.

# RED WINE SAUCE

*Fish bones are easily available at the fish counter of your grocery store. We like Knorr brand seafood stock concentrate (usually found in the soup aisle of your grocery store), but other brands can also be used.*

1 lb. fish bones
¼ cup (½ stick) butter
1 small carrot, minced
½ cup chopped onion
¼ tsp. dried thyme
1 bay leaf

4 parsley stems
2 tsp. crushed peppercorns
1 cup red wine
1 cup *Fish Stock*, page 126
1 tsp. seafood stock concentrate
½ tsp. anchovy paste, optional

Rinse fish bones, discard any fins or tail, and chop bones. Set aside. Melt butter in a large heavy saucepan over low heat. Add carrot and onion and cook for 5 minutes, stirring occasionally. Add thyme, bay leaf, parsley stems, fish bones and peppercorns. Cover and cook for 10 minutes. Raise heat to medium and add wine and *Fish Stock*. Cook sauce, uncovered, for 10 minutes. Skim off any foam or fat that rises to the surface. Season with seafood stock concentrate. Bring sauce to a boil, reduce heat to low and simmer for 5 minutes. Pour sauce through a strainer, pressing solids to extract all the sauce. Discard solids and stir anchovy paste, if using, into the sauce. Serve hot.

# SWEET AND SOUR MAYONNAISE

*Serve this sauce with hot poached salmon.*

1/2 cup (1 stick) butter, softened

2 tsp. dry mustard

5 tbs. sugar

3/4 cup white vinegar

4 eggs

Beat together butter, mustard, sugar, vinegar and eggs in a heavy saucepan. Place over medium heat and cook, whisking constantly, until mixture boils. Serve immediately.

# DILL MUSTARD SAUCE

*This sauce can be made 2 or 3 days ahead. Serve with gravlax or cold poached salmon.*

1 cup Dijon mustard or yellow mustard

1 cup sour cream

1/2 cup chopped fresh dill

Mix ingredients together in a bowl. Cover and refrigerate until ready to use.

# TARRAGON HONEY-MUSTARD DRESSING

Makes 1½ cups

*Prepared up to a day ahead, this sweet and pungent dressing can be used with cold salmon served on a bed of lettuce.*

¼ cup extra-virgin olive oil
1½ tbs. white wine vinegar
2 tbs. Dijon mustard
1 tsp. honey
1 clove garlic, minced
1 tbs. chopped fresh tarragon, or 1 tsp. dried
salt and pepper to taste

Combine oil, vinegar, mustard, honey, garlic and tarragon in a blender container. Blend until smooth. Season with salt and pepper.

# BASIC MAYONNAISE

*Homemade mayonnaise is delicious and not too difficult to make.*

3 egg yolks
2 tbs. white wine vinegar
2 tbs. lemon juice
2 tbs. water

1 tbs. Dijon mustard
$\frac{1}{2}$ tsp. salt
$\frac{1}{4}$ tsp. cayenne pepper
3 cups vegetable oil

Place a small saucepan containing 1 inch of water over low heat and bring to a simmer. Combine egg yolks, vinegar, lemon juice and water in a stainless steel bowl. Place the bowl over the pan of simmering water. Whisk egg yolk mixture constantly until it reaches 150° on an instant-read thermometer, about 1 minute; the egg mixture should be creamy and thick. Immediately remove bowl from heat. Cool egg mixture to room temperature.

To egg mixture, add mustard, salt and cayenne. Using an electric mixer on low speed, beat in oil. Start with 1 teaspoon at a time, and as oil is incorporated, pour in a thin steady stream as you are beating. Continue beating until all oil has been added and mayonnaise is thick. Thin with more lemon juice, if desired. Store in the refrigerator for up to 4 weeks.

# MAYONNAISE VARIATIONS

**ANCHOVY MAYONNAISE:** Finely chop 2 oz. anchovy fillets. Combine with 1 tsp. minced garlic, 1 tbs. chopped parsley and 1 cup mayonnaise.

**ANDALOUSE SAUCE:** To 1 cup mayonnaise, add 3 tbs. tomato paste, 2 tbs. diced pimientos, 1 tsp. lemon juice and $1/2$ tsp. Worcestershire sauce.

**CHANTILLY SAUCE:** To 2 cups mayonnaise, add 1 tbs. lemon juice, 1 tsp. hot pepper sauce and $1/2$ cup whipped cream.

**ANDALOUSE SAUCE:** Combine 1 cup mayonnaise, $3/4$ cup fresh basil and 1 tbs. lemon juice in a food processor workbowl and blend. Season with salt and pepper.

**COCKTAIL SAUCE:** Combine $11/2$ cups mayonnaise, $1/2$ cup chili sauce, 1 tbs. ketchup, 1 tsp. Worcestershire sauce, 1 tbs. lemon juice, $1/4$ tsp. seasoned salt and $1/4$ tsp. paprika.

**NEW ORLEANS SAUCE:** Combine $11/4$ cups mayonnaise, $11/2$ tsp. curry powder, 1 tbs. lemon juice, $1/2$ cup ketchup and $1/2$ cup sour cream.

**TOMATO-BASIL MAYONNAISE:** Combine 1 cup mayonnaise, 1 tbs. tomato paste, 3 tbs. chopped fresh basil, 2 tbs. cooked, diced red bell pepper and 1 dash Tabasco Sauce.

# CREAMY CUCUMBER DRESSING

Makes 1½ cups

*Serve this with cold poached salmon or smoked salmon.*

1 cup peeled shredded cucumber
½ tsp. salt
½ cup sour cream

½ cup mayonnaise
2 tsp. chopped fresh dill, or 1 tsp. dried
¼ tsp. pepper

Combine cucumber and salt in a colander; set aside to drain for 1 hour. Squeeze cucumber dry, place in a bowl and mix with sour cream, mayonnaise, dill and pepper.

# CREAMY GARLIC SAUCE

Makes 1 cup

*Try this sauce with cold poached salmon, or as a dressing for pasta salad.*

½ cup sour cream
½ cup mayonnaise
3 tbs. wine vinegar
2 tbs. olive oil
1 tsp. sugar

salt and pepper to taste
1 tbs. chopped fresh tarragon, or 1 tsp.
  dried
4 cloves garlic, minced

Combine all ingredients in a blender container and blend at high speed until creamy.

# MAYONNAISE MUSTARD SAUCE

*This sauce enhances any cold salmon dish.*

½ cup white wine
1 tsp. chopped shallots or onion
1 tbs. mustard seeds

1 cup mayonnaise
2 tsp. Dijon mustard

Combine wine, shallots and mustard seeds in a non-aluminum saucepan over high heat and bring to a boil. Cook until liquid is reduced by three-fourths. Set aside to cool.

In a bowl, stir cooled shallot mixture into mayonnaise. Add mustard. Press sauce through a strainer and refrigerate until ready to use.

# PAPRIKA MAYONNAISE

*This mayonnaise is very good with cold egg dishes, artichokes, zucchini and potatoes, as well as with poached salmon.*

1 clove garlic, minced
½ tsp. paprika
2 cups mayonnaise
1 tbs. mustard
½ tsp. salt
¼ tsp. pepper
½ cup diced ham

In a bowl, combine garlic, paprika and mayonnaise. Fold in mustard. Season with salt and pepper and add diced ham. Refrigerate until ready to use.

# REMOULADE SAUCE

*This classic sauce is delicious with deep-fried fish and cold meats.*

3 oz. sour pickles
1 tbs. tiny capers, drained
2 anchovy fillets
1 tbs. Dijon mustard
2 cups mayonnaise
1 tbs. minced fresh parsley
½ tbs. minced fresh chervil, or ½ tsp. dried
½ tbs. minced fresh tarragon, or ½ tsp. dried
1 tsp. salt
¼ tsp. pepper

Finely chop pickles, capers and anchovies; fold into mustard, mayonnaise, parsley, chervil, tarragon, salt and pepper in a large bowl. Refrigerate until ready to use.

# SAUCE VERTE (GREEN SAUCE)

*This lovely green sauce is fragrant with herbs.*

1 cup mayonnaise, divided
1 tbs. lemon juice
$1/2$ cup chopped fresh spinach
$1/2$ cup chopped fresh parsley
$1/2$ cup chopped watercress
1 tbs. chopped fresh chives
1 tbs. chopped fresh dill, or 1 tsp. dried
2 tsp. chopped fresh tarragon, or 1 tsp. dried
salt and pepper to taste

Combine $1/2$ cup of the mayonnaise in a blender container with lemon juice, spinach, parsley and watercress. Blend until smooth. Pour into a small bowl. Add remaining $1/2$ cup mayonnaise, chives, dill, tarragon, salt and pepper. Blend well. Cover and refrigerate until ready to use.

# TARTAR SAUCE

*This new and improved version of the classic tartar sauce really shines when served with fried salmon.*

2 hard-cooked eggs
1 tbs. chopped fresh chives
1 medium shallot, chopped, or 2 tbs. chopped onion
1 tsp. chopped fresh tarragon, or ½ tsp. dried
1 tsp. chopped fresh chervil, or ½ tsp. dried
1 tsp. chopped fresh parsley
1 cup mayonnaise
½ tsp. salt
¼ tsp. pepper
1 tsp. lemon juice

Peel eggs and chop in a food processor workbowl. Place in a bowl and combine with chives, shallot, tarragon, chervil, parsley and mayonnaise. Season with salt, pepper and lemon juice. Refrigerate until ready to use.

# TYROLIENNE SAUCE

*This sauce elevates the flavor of a poached fillet of salmon.*

1/4 cup chopped tomatoes
1 cup mayonnaise
1 tbs. chopped fresh parsley
1 tbs. chopped fresh chervil, or 1 tsp. dried

1/8 tsp. pepper
1/4 tsp. Worcestershire sauce
1 tsp. chili sauce

Place tomatoes in a small saucepan over medium heat and cook until they are reduced to a thick consistency. Set aside to cool.

In a bowl, combine tomatoes, mayonnaise, parsley, chervil, pepper, Worcestershire and chili sauce. Refrigerate until ready to use.

# BLACK BEAN AND MANGO SALSA

*This colorful tropical salsa is especially good with* Honey-Lime Salmon Fillets, *page 73.*

2 tsp. olive oil
1 cup chopped red onion
1 jalapeño pepper, minced
2 cans (15 oz. each) black beans, rinsed and drained
1 cup diced mangoes
1 tsp. dried coriander
1 tsp. ground cumin
2 tbs. white wine vinegar
½ cup chopped fresh cilantro

Heat oil in a nonstick pan over medium-high heat until very hot. Sauté onion until it begins to soften. Add jalapeño and sauté for 1 minute. Stir in beans and mangoes. Reduce heat to medium-low and simmer for 5 minutes. Add coriander, cumin and vinegar. Heat through. Stir in cilantro. Serve hot or cold.

# SALSA VERDE

*This tart green salsa will keep up to a week in the refrigerator.*

12 tomatillos
2 cups fresh cilantro
2 jalapeño peppers, seeded and chopped
$1/4$ tsp. salt

Peel papery husks off tomatillos and discard. Rinse tomatillos and put them in a saucepan with water just to cover. Bring to a boil over high heat, reduce heat to low and simmer until tomatillos are soft, about 5 minutes. Remove tomatillos and reserve $1/2$ cup cooking liquid.

In a food processor workbowl or blender container, puree tomatillos, reserved cooking liquid, cilantro, jalapeños and salt. Refrigerate until ready to use.

# PESTO SAUCE

Makes about 1 cup

*Before the arrival of food processors, basil, garlic and nuts were ground together with a mortar and pestle, hence the word "pesto." This pesto sauce is full of flavor and has less oil than most recipes. Serve with poached, baked or grilled salmon.*

$\frac{1}{2}$ cup pine nuts (pignoli)
6 cloves garlic, minced
1 cup fresh basil leaves
$\frac{1}{2}$ cup grated Parmesan cheese
$\frac{1}{2}$ cup extra-virgin olive oil
pepper to taste

In a food processor workbowl, pulse pine nuts, garlic, basil, Parmesan and oil until blended and smooth. Season with pepper.

Refrigerate pesto for up to a week, or freeze for up to 6 weeks.

### MAYONNAISE PESTO SAUCE

Makes 2 cups

For a nice variation that goes well with poached salmon, stir in $\frac{1}{2}$ cup mayonnaise to prepared pesto sauce. Add more mayonnaise to desired consistency and taste.

# INDEX

Anchovy mayonnaise 141
Andalouse sauce 141
Appetizers and hors d'oeuvres 14-34
Apricot-horseradish sauce with salmon steaks 86
Arctic char 2
Asian salmon, grilled with Japanese eggplant 72
Atlantic salmon 1

Baked salmon fillets 63
Baked whole salmon 100
Basil
    -dressed baby greens with smoked salmon 37
    sauce with salmon fillets 64
    -tomato mayonnaise 141
Bechamel sauce (cream sauce) 128
Beurre blanc (white butter sauce) 127
Black bean and mango salsa 149
Blinis 21
Blueback salmon, braised with white wine sauce
    102
Bouillon, court 125
Brochettes of salmon 58
Brook trout 2
Bruschetta on rye, smoked salmon 17
Burgers, salmon 60
Butter sauce, white (beurre blanc) 127
Butter sauce with salmon croquettes 56
Butterfly fillets 4

Cajun salmon fillet with angel hair pasta 42
Cakes, salmon 61
Caper-riesling sauce with salmon 81
Capers with smoked salmon spread 27
Casserole, creamed salmon 116

Champagne sauce with salmon steaks 96
Chantilly sauce 141
Chinook salmon 1
Chives with cream sauce 134
Chowder, corn and salmon 62
Chum salmon 2
Cocktail sauce 141
Coho salmon 1
Cold poached salmon steaks 90
Cold salmon and pasta 44
Contaminants in salmon 3
Corn chowder and salmon 62
Corncakes, smoked salmon 24
Court bouillon 125
Cream
    ginger with broiled fillets of salmon 65
    sauce with chives 134
    sauce with whole salmon 110
Creamed fettuccine with smoked salmon 40
Creamy cucumber dressing 142
Creamy garlic sauce 142
Creme fraiche, dill with smoked salmon and pota-
    to galettes 22
Crepes, smoked salmon 52
Croque monsieur, smoked salmon 53
Croquettes, salmon with butter sauce 56

Crust
    horseradish-ginger with salmon fillets 68
    mustard-honey with salmon 69
    potato with fillets of salmon 66
    salmon-in-a 118
Cucumber(s)
    dressing, creamy 142

paprika sauce 135
salad with smoked salmon 19
stuffed 20
Cured salmon 6
Cutlets, salmon Pojarsky 117

Dill
    creme fraiche with smoked salmon and potato
        galettes 22
    -mustard grilled salmon fillet 71
    mustard sauce 138
    piccata sauce 133
Drawn salmon 3
Dressed salmon 3
Dressing, creamy cucumber 142
Dressing, tarragon honey-mustard 139

Eggplant, Japanese with grilled Asian salmon 72
Eggs, salmon-stuffed 34

Fennel with braised salmon steaks 88
Fettuccine, creamed with smoked salmon 40
Fettuccine with smoked salmon sauce 41
Fillets 4
Fish seasoning 43
Fish stock 126
Florentine, salmon 120
Freezing salmon 5

Garlic
    roasted with salmon 70
    -red pepper sauce 136
    sauce, creamy 142

**Ginger**
cream with broiled fillets of salmon 65
-horseradish crust, salmon fillets in 68
ratatouille with salmon 87
Glazing salmon 5
Gougeonettes of salmon 59
Gravlax 14
Gravlax, Scandanavian 7
Grilled salmon salad 38
Grilled salmon skewers 26

Hazelnut sauce 131
Hollandaise sauce 130
Hollandaise sauce variations 131
**Honey**
-lime salmon fillets 73
-mustard crust with salmon 69
-mustard tarragon dressing 139
**Horseradish**
-apricot sauce with salmon steaks 86
-ginger crust, salmon fillets in 68
-mustard vinaigrette with salmon fillets 84
Hot-smoked salmon 6
Hot-smoking salmon at home 10
Hot-smoking salmon with a grill 11

Japanese eggplant with grilled Asian salmon 72

Kedgeree of salmon 49
King salmon 1
Kippered salmon 6

Lake trout 2
Lemon-rice stuffing with grilled whole salmon 104
Lentils with salmon roast 98
Lime-honey salmon fillets 73
Lox 7

Macadamia sauce 131
Maltaise sauce 131
Mango and black bean salsa 149
**Marinade**
Asian salmon 123
basic salmon 123
spicy salmon 124
Marinades and sauces 123-151
Matelote of salmon 112
Maximilian sauce 131
**Mayonnaise**
basic 140
mustard sauce 143
paprika 144
pesto sauce 151
sweet and sour 138
tomato-basil 141
variations 141

Mayonnaise, watercress with poached salmon 75
Mornay sauce 132
Mousse, cold salmon 28
Mousseline sauce 131
Moutarde sauce 131
**Mustard**
-dill grilled salmon fillet 71
dill sauce 138
-honey crust with salmon 69
-honey tarragon dressing 139
-horseradish vinaigrette with salmon fillets 84
mayonnaise sauce 143
-parsley sauce with poached salmon steaks 92

Napa Valley Steelhead 107
New Orleans sauce 141
Nova lox 7

Nova Scotia smoked salmon 7
Nova smoked salmon 7

Omelet, smoked salmon 50

Pacific salmon 1
Pacific salmon steaks, broiled with salsa butter 89
Pan-smoked salmon 55
Paprika cucumber sauce 135
Paprika mayonnaise 144
Parsley-mustard sauce with poached salmon
steaks 92
**Pasta**
angel hair with Cajun salmon fillet 42
and cold salmon 44
and salmon salad Suzanne 45
summer salmon 46
Pastas and salads 36-46
Pesto sauce 151
Pesto sauce, mayonnaise 151
Phyllo-wrapped salmon 76
Pine nut-crusted salmon 74
Pink salmon 2
Pizza, smoked salmon 51
Potato crust, fillets of salmon in 66
Potato galettes with smoked salmon and dill
creme fraiche 22
Provencale, salmon 121

Quesadillas, smoked salmon 16

Rainbow trout 2
Ratatouille, ginger with salmon 87
Red pepper-garlic sauce 136
Red wine sauce 137
Red wine sauce, salmon in 79
Remoulade sauce 145

Rice-lemon stuffing with grilled whole salmon 104
Riesling-caper sauce with salmon 81
Rillettes of salmon 29
Roast, salmon 4

**Salad**
  cucumber with smoked salmon 19
  grilled salmon 38
  salmon 39
  salmon Suzanne and pasta 45
  smoked salmon spinach 36
Salads and pasta 36-46
**Salmon**
  Atlantic 1
  bagelettes, smoked 15
  baked fillets 63
  baked whole 100
  bonne femme 77
  braised Blueback with white wine sauce 102
  brochettes of 58
  broiled fillets with ginger cream 65
  burgers 60
  buying fresh 4
  cakes 61
  Chinook 1
  Chum 2
  Coho 1
  cold, and pasta 44
  cold poached steaks 90
  contaminants 3
  and corn chowder 62
  creamed casserole 116
  croquettes with butter sauce 56
  cured 6
  cutlets Pojarsky 117
  drawn 3
  dressed 3

en croute 78
fillet, Cajun with angel hair pasta 42
fillets 4
fillets in a horseradish-ginger crust 68
fillets in potato crust 66
fillets with basil sauce 64
fillets with mustard-horseradish vinaigrette 84
Florentine 120
freezing 5
with ginger ratatouille 87
glazing 5
gougeonettes of 59
grilled Asian with Japanese eggplant 72
grilled mustard-dill fillet 71
grilled whole with lemon-rice stuffing 104
handling and storing 5
and health 2-3
honey-lime fillets 73
hot-smoking at home 10
in red wine sauce 79
in-a-crust 118
jerky 8
kedgeree of 49
King 1
matelote of 112
mousse, cold 28
with mustard-honey crust 69
Pacific 1
pan-smoked 55
pasta, summer 46
phyllo-wrapped 76
pine nut-crusted 74
Pink 2
poached steaks with mustard-parsley sauce 92
poached with watercress mayonnaise 75
Provencale 121
with riesling-caper sauce 81

rillettes of 29
roast 4
roast with lentils 98
with roasted garlic 70
salad 39
salad, grilled 38
salad Suzanne and pasta 45
seared with Thai vegetables 82
shrimp terrine 31
Silver 1
skewers, grilled 26
smoked 6-8
smoking in a wok 12
Sockeye 2
species 1-2
steaks 3
steaks, braised with fennel 88
steaks en papillote 94
steaks in Champagne sauce 96
steaks in white wine sauce 91
steaks Italienne 95
steaks, Pacific broiled with salsa butter 89
steaks with apricot-horseradish sauce 86
Steelhead 2
-stuffed eggs 34
stuffed fillet 85
teriyaki 80
terrine of 32
tortillas 97
tournedos of 106
whole roasted with wild rice stuffing 108
whole with cream sauce 110
and wild rice pie 114
Salmon entrees 49-121
Salsa, black bean and mango 149
Salsa butter with broiled Pacific salmon steaks 89
Salsa verde 150

**Sauce**
andalouse 141
apricot-horseradish with salmon steaks 86
basil with salmon fillets 64
bechamel (cream sauce) 128
butter, with salmon croquettes 56
Champagne, with salmon steaks 96
Chantilly 141
cocktail 141
cream, with chives 134
cream with whole salmon 110
creamy garlic 142
cucumber paprika 135
dill mustard 138
dill piccata 133
hazelnut 131
Hollandaise 130
Hollandaise variations 131
macadamia 131
Maltaise 131
maximilian 131
mayonnaise mustard 143
mayonnaise pesto 151
mornay 132
mousseline 131
moutarde 131
mustard-parsley with poached salmon steaks 92
New Orleans 141
pesto 151
red pepper-garlic 136
red wine 137
remoulade 145
riesling-caper with salmon 81
salmon in red wine 79
smoked salmon with fettuccine 41
tartar 147

Tyrolienne 148
veloute 129
verte (green sauce) 146
white butter (beurre blanc) 127
white wine with braised Blueback salmon 102
white wine with salmon steaks 91
Sauces and marinades 123-151
Seasoning, fish 43
Shrimp salmon terrine 31
Silver salmon 1
**Smoked salmon**
and dill creme fraiche with potato galettes 22
bagelettes 15
with basil-dressed baby greens 37
bruschetta on rye 17
buying 8-9
corncakes 24
with creamed fettuccine 40
crepes 52
croque monsieur 53
with cucumber salad 19
omelet 50
pizza 51
quesadillas 16
souffle 54
spinach salad 36
spirals 25
spread with capers 27
tartare 18
terrine 30
Smoked salmon 6
Smoking salmon in a wok 12
Sockeye salmon 2
Souffle, smoked salmon 54
Spinach, in salmon Florentine 120
Spinach salad, smoked salmon 36
Spread, smoked salmon with capers 27

Steelhead Napa Valley 107
Steelhead salmon 2
Stock, fish 126
Storing and handling salmon 5
Stuffed salmon fillet 85
Stuffing, lemon-rice with grilled whole salmon 104
Stuffing, wild rice with whole roasted salmon 108
Sweet and sour mayonnaise 138

Tarragon honey-mustard dressing 139
Tartar sauce 147
Teriyaki salmon 80
Terrine
of salmon 32
salmon shrimp 31
smoked salmon 30
Thai vegetables 83
Tomato-basil mayonnaise 141
Tortillas, salmon 97
Tournedos of salmon 106
Tyrolienne sauce 148

Vegetables, Thai with seared salmon 82
Veloute sauce 129
Verde, salsa 150
Verte, sauce (green sauce) 146
Vinaigrette, mustard-horseradish with salmon fillets 84

Watercress mayonnaise with poached salmon 75
White wine sauce with braised Blueback salmon 102
Wild Baltic smoked salmon 7
Wild rice pie and salmon 114
Wild rice stuffing with whole roasted salmon 108
Wild Western nova smoked salmon 7

# Serve Creative, Easy, Nutritious Meals with **nitty gritty®** Cookbooks

1 or 2, Cooking for
100 Dynamite Desserts
9 x 13 Pan Cookbook
Asian Cooking
Bagels, Best
Barbecue Cookbook
Beer and Good Food
Big Book Bread Machine
Big Book Kitchen Appliance
Big Book Snack, Appetizer
Blender Drinks
Bread Baking
New Bread Machine Book
Bread Machine III
Bread Machine V
Bread Machine VI
Bread Machine, Entrees
Burger Bible
Cappuccino/Espresso
Casseroles
Chicken, Unbeatable
Chile Peppers
Cooking in Clay

Coffee and Tea
Convection Oven
Cook-Ahead Cookbook
Crockery Pot, Extra-Special
Deep Fryer
Dehydrator Cookbook
Dessert Fondues
Edible Gifts
Edible Pockets
Fabulous Fiber Cookery
Fondue and Hot Dips
Fondue, New International
Freezer, 'Fridge, Pantry
Garlic Cookbook
Grains, Cooking with
Healthy Cooking on Run
Ice Cream Maker
Indoor Grill, Cooking on
Irish Pub Cooking
Italian, Quick and Easy
Juicer Book II
Kids, Cooking with Your
Kids, Healthy Snacks for

Loaf Pan, Recipes for
Low-Carb
No Salt No Sugar No Fat
Party Foods/Appetizers
Pasta Machine Cookbook
Pasta, Quick and Easy
Pinch of Time
Pizza, Best
Porcelain, Cooking in
Pressure Cooker
Rice Cooker
Salmon Cookbook
Sandwich Maker
Simple Substitutions
Slow Cooking
Slow Cooker, Vegetarian
Soups and Stews
Soy & Tofu Recipes
Tapas Fantásticas
Toaster Oven Cookbook
Waffles & Pizzelles
Wedding Catering book
Wraps and Roll-Ups

"Millions of books sold—for more than 35 years"   For a free catalog, call: Bristol Publishing Enterprises
(800) 346-4889
www.bristolpublishing.com